Trail of the Dove

Trail of the Dove

HOW A MOTHER AND HER GROWN SON

LEARNED TO LOVE EACH OTHER ON A

CROSS-COUNTRY MOTORCYCLE JOURNEY

Dorothy Friedman

COUNCIL OAK BOOKS

SAN FRANCISCO / TULSA

Council Oak Books, LLC

1290 Chestnut Street, Suite 2, San Francisco, CA 94109

1350 E. 15th Street, Tulsa, OK 74120

TRAIL OF THE DOVE: *How a Mother and Her Grown Son*

Learned to Love Each Other on a Cross-Country Motorcycle Journey.

Library of Congress Cataloging-in-Publication Data

Friedman, Dorothy.
    Trail of the dove : how a mother and her grown son learned to love each
other on a cross-country motorcycle journey / Dorothy Friedman.—1st ed.
        p. cm.
    ISBN 1-57178-089-0
        1. Friedman, Dorothy. 2. Friedman, David. 3. Motorcyclists—United
States—Biography. 4. Mothers and sons—United States. I. Title.

GV1060.2.F75 A3 2000

                                                        99-089865

First edition / First printing.

Printed in Canada

00 01 02 03 04 05 06   5   4   3   2   1

"Long ago I lost a hound,
a bay horse, and a turtle dove
and have been on their trail ever since."
HENRY DAVID THOREAU

The Initiate

May your union be blessed with children to sustain you in your old age…

Late June, Los Angeles, CA

When I answer the phone, his voice is like the mountain air of British Columbia where he has made his home: clear, refreshing, and quite unexpected in these parts. "If you still want to make that trip, you're on. We'll be going to the BMW rally in South Dakota. The Dove and I have discussed it, and we both agree."

The Dove—"for the way it sails through the curves"—is a BMW motorcycle, and while the personification here is facetious, the relationship between this man and his machine is no joking matter.

"So how about it?"

I'm stunned momentarily. I've hoped for something like this but…

Two years ago a painful rift developed between David and me. Bad enough that I was still learning to cope with the problems of advancing age and widowhood, but then this had to happen. David is the younger of my two sons; the cause of the rift was a woman he was seeing. It wasn't the first time I'd disapproved of his choice of companions. But it was the first time it seriously threatened our relationship; Barbie had all but banned me from his home. It hit me like an earthquake, like a betrayal of the very ground beneath my feet. Because I still loved him, I needed him. But because I was so angry over the incident, I found it impossible to tell him so.

"You still there, Ma?"

"I'm still here." *Just thinking, David.*

The impasse persisted. In the last two years I had seen him only once, for just a few hours, as he passed through L.A. on his way to the Florida Keys. I let it drop then, almost in a whisper, that I wished I could go along—if not this time, then maybe the next. I wasn't even sure at the time that he had even heard me: his reply was vague. Now here he was, finally after all this time, asking me along on one of his adventures, a wish too much to hope for coming true, and I'm grousing to myself over water two years under the bridge.

"Ma?"

Now who am I fooling? I'm sixty-eight years old; I suffer from an arthritic knee; my circulation is so poor that I sometimes find Southern California winters trying; the thought of mounting a bicycle is terrifying enough, let alone a motorcycle.

"Ma, I need an answer…"

"Of course I'll come!"

He fills me in with some of the details: The BMW Motorcycle Owners of America National Rally is held annually at different locations around the U.S. and draws enthusiasts from all around the world. "We'll be doing a lot of camping, and the riding won't always be easy. I've mapped our route almost exclusively on secondary highways, the twistier the better. It'll be tough," I'm properly forewarned.

"So what? I'm still tough," I assure him, hamming it up, flexing a bicep he can't see, quite ecstatic really at the invitation. "Besides, all that matters is that we're together again."

There is a lull in the conversation, just time enough for both of us to entertain second thoughts. Then I say, "If you really want me to come... You're sure, David?"

"Of course I'm sure, or I wouldn't have asked," he says without hesitation. "I'll be in Los Angeles Friday, the sixth of July. We'll leave the following morning. Pack light, just a few warm things—okay, Ma?"

When I hang up, I let out one peach of a sigh, and with it goes not quite all the shored-up pain of what happened between us two years earlier. Still, after all this time, a whole month together again with my son!

FRIDAY, JULY 6, LOS ANGELES, CA

The last thing David has told me before he hangs up is to let my friends know I'll be gone about a month. Of course, when I mention the motorcycle, their collective reaction is predictable: "At your age?!"

"Well," I have to say, "what about my age? I'm not getting any younger, you know. It's now or never."

To my doctor I say, "A stroke, a heart attack, cancer—that I'm afraid of. Riding behind my son on a motorcycle, I'm not."

He smiles. He knows me too well. "Who's going to stop you?" he says with a shrug.

The whole week before we leave, I promise myself that this time I'm going to hold my tongue, neither provoke nor offend, leave the nag at home.

Friday evening arrives at last. The aroma of David's favorite, my potato pudding, fills the apartment. Anxiously I wait, keenly listening for the *putt-putt* idling sound of the Dove—David's considerate habit of walking the bike quietly to the door—and when I do, I rush down the stairs and into his arms.

In the glow of the street lamp illuminating his mobile face, his eyes sparkle. People have said he has the head of Christ. He has since shaved off his beard.

After dinner, after the dishes are done, David is just about to step out to see some friends in the area. Very appreciative, just as he always was as a child (especially when I managed not to burn the roast), he gives me a hug in the kitchen. "Thanks, Ma. That was great."

Then with his hands on my shoulders, he feels he has to remind me, "We'll be on the bike in all kinds of weather." He pauses, his eyes searching mine. "Are you sure?"

"If you're sure, I'm sure," I say, reassuring us both.

SATURDAY, JULY 7, PHOENIX, AZ

Despite not sleeping well—up until past three, worried sick, waiting for David to come home—I feel fine this morning. The die is cast, the moment is now. Our sleeping bags, inflatables, and clothing are all neatly packed in the removable cases flanking the rear wheel of the motorcycle. The fairing pocket, which incorporates a fiberglass shield, contains my high-blood-pressure pills, vitamins, lipstick, and a white feather, for luck. Or in case I lose my nerve.

Somehow in all the excitement I have managed to forget such superfluities as my toothbrush, hairbrush, and dental floss. When I go back for them, I notice the plants and hope that my neighbor will remember to water them.

The only things I have made a point of leaving behind are the aspirin, the boredom, and the cobwebs.

I take one last look at my apartment, at my paintings done so many years ago at the Brooklyn Museum—before Leo's illness, which postponed any professional artistic aspirations. Then I'm rushing down the stairs to the street where David sits on the Dove, balancing it with one foot.

"Are you sure you have everything you need?" he double-checks.

"Of course not. You ought to know better than to ask me that!"

David laughs. "Ma, if there's an emergency and the intercom is off, tap my right shoulder three times. If it can wait, tap my left shoulder twice."

My right foot on the peg, I mount the bike for the first

time, easily swinging my left leg over the back. David suggests that I do it the opposite way. I tell him I can't because my right knee is arthritic. At that, he turns and I see a brief shadow stealing across his face. I chase away any doubts, his or mine; I'm too thrilled with anticipation of this great adventure to entertain the negatives.

My resolve is short-lived. In the next instant I'm already complaining, albeit half good-naturedly, about the helmet, which is much too big for my head. "Do I have to wear this? It's like putting my head in a cement mixer." I'm tugging at the leather gloves. "David, really. Leathers in the desert in July?"

"The gloves will keep your hands cool. The leathers are for protection, in case of a fall. And you know you have to wear the helmet."

My neighbor Emily appears in her bathrobe to see us off. Like the rest, she has her doubts; do they conceal envy? I wonder. "Come back safe and sound," she says, waving good-bye as David revs the engine and the Dove springs forward.

"*This royal plot, this land, this earth, this realm,*" I intone.

"*This England!*" David finishes the line. "Next to godliness, Ma, Shakespeare," he laughs again.

Experienced from the back of a motorcycle, the city becomes a blurry montage of sights and sounds: horns, sirens, vegetable-dyed mohawks, the gray pavement of the streets running beneath us, the homeless beginning to stir to life on the gray, concrete benches. We cruise through the suburbs with their pleasant ranch-style homes, freshly mowed lawns, leashed dogs, the children shouting behind the fences that encircle the swimming pools. A man is painting his house a soft, warm yellow.

Overhead flies a flock of birds in perfect formation, with no more need of a compass than we. I savor my anticipated joy. This is genuine luxury, this wild sense of continuity with the air, the sky, the sun; the sensation is almost erotic. The gypsy in me is set free once more.

I have set aside an imaginary jug, to be filled with twenty-four hours of perfect minutes. These are the first.

With the desert stretching before us, the landscape has begun to run flat. It's maddeningly hot, the heat manifesting itself as a golden haze brushed unevenly across the sky.

"Flowering time in the desert," David says over the intercom.

I nod absentmindedly. Our first destination is Phoenix and Mark's home. I'm looking forward to this, as I do all our visits. Older son and a psychology professor, Mark is also my friend and advisor.

But that's miles and miles away. As the Dove flies down Interstate 10 through the endless desert at 85 mph, maybe faster (I don't dare look at the speedometer)—rushing past Riverside, Palm Springs, Indio with its stands of rugs, dates, Native American artifacts—the searing, golden heat begins to blur my vision; I'm perspiring heavily beneath the clunky helmet.

By the time we reach Blythe, I'm completely dehydrated; my lips are dry and cracked, parched as the desert. My helmet feels like a large price on my head. My attention becomes fixated on the wisps of curly hair escaping from beneath David's helmet; I'm a transistor radio with a broken receiver. The heat is shorting my circuits and it's only my first day!

I have sworn to myself that I am not going to be a burden. But now I can't help it. The heat of the sun is curdling me; my head is bowed almost in an attitude of penance.

Luckily we've made a pit stop for gas. I find a rusty old tap and slide my head under it, keeping it there until I see David is ready to leave.

The respite, however, is too brief. Back on the road, I soon realize that I'm beginning to black out. I give David the three-tap signal on the right shoulder and he immediately pulls off the highway at a rest area. He attempts to speak to me over the intercom, but my ringing ears drown out his words. When we pull up on the grass—David being considerate again; this way they can bury me where I fall—I can barely make it off the bike. With effort I weave straight-backed toward the rest room. Once inside my knees buckle and I sink to the floor. Everything has gone black. I know I'm causing a scene, but I couldn't care less. After all, I'm dying.

A woman brings me a wet towel; another gives me a bottle of Gatorade, which I'm too sick to drink. "Is the motorcyclist your ... traveling companion?" the latter asks delicately.

"My son. Please tell him I'm all right."

She looks at me in disbelief. *Yes, yes, I know. At my age!*

After a while, still fighting off unconsciousness, I all but crawl outside, where David meets me and helps me into the shade of a picnic shelter. By now I'm ready for CPR, *but not from my son, oh please God, not him.* With his chamois cloth he towels down as much of me as decently possible, and then applies ice to my neck, back, and head. I look gratefully up into his face. His green eyes are sympathetic, but they seem to betray something else: misgivings, I think.

"Ma," he addresses me gently, "I think we should find a motel and when you're feeling better, I'll put you on a train or a bus."

"No," I insist. "No, I'm not ready to give in. I'm going to see those Rockies if..." My words have trailed off. "David, we're already past Blythe and Mark is waiting. Just give me a little time. Please. Don't send me home."

My hands still feel clammy. David rubs them to restore circulation, brushes the hair away from my eyes, and wipes my face with the cool cloth. A wry-looking, leathery-faced man in a cowboy hat comes up with a pitcher of ice. "If you're gonna ride a motorcycle in one-hundred-and-twenty-degree heat, better make sure it's air-conditioned. People been known to die in heat like this."

David is nodding his head slowly. "He's right, Ma. I've been through here before, stopped everywhere there was water, drank it, poured it over my head, my chest, even filled my boots, my gloves with it. It's my fault. I should have known better."

As David and I sit together, waiting for my spell to pass, the sky begins to darken above the horizon. There follows a distant rumble, and I find myself praying hard: *Dear God, please, a miracle. Let it rain.*

It isn't long before slashes of lightning and the crack of thunder are accompanied by a whipping wind and needles of rain. The sweet, wet smell reinvigorates me. I strap my helmet back on and climb on the bike behind David.

"You all right?" he turns around and asks.

"Sure." And to make it more convincing, I flash him my bravest smile.

The rain is coming down in dense torrents—much more than I prayed for. Visibility is so poor David tucks in behind a transport truck and turns the emergency flashers on. We pass cars by the dozen stopped on the shoulder to wait out the storm. But not David. We must be doing 85 mph again, this time into a flaying wind and a driving rain that rebounds a foot high after hitting the pavement. The desert appears to be flooding. I'm terrified, but not my son, with his steady eye and steady hand, and a relentless timetable to keep.

This terror takes me back to the first night after Leo was laid in the ground. I came home and refused to lock the door, unable to face the rest of my life alone. I cried hysterically, imagining his reaction to his exposure to the pitiless elements, the loneliness and fear of a soul that refuses to leave its body. *Rest in peace, my beloved, even while you were cheated out of half a lifetime.*

We ride out of the rain, but the wind continues to blow mightily. Before long, the desert around us is dry again—just as we've begun to dry—and the wind now has begun to pick up the dust. First we see the dust storm ahead; then we're in it. No worries, I feel fine, and just feeling fine right now is enough.

When the dust storm subsides ten miles later, it's early evening, pink and calm, but my demon son of speed insists now upon passing cars four, five at a time! Why? Where's the finish line? He's already confessed to racking up one speeding ticket on his way down to L.A.

Then trouble: as he tries to pass an eighteen-wheeler, the driver begins crossing over into our lane. I nearly roll backward off the bike as David has to accelerate to a terrific speed to pass, with just enough room to make it back safely into the right lane. We must be doing 100 mph now! I pound him on the back with both fists. While this is not part of the code, he gets the message and slows to 95 or so.

We pull off at a restaurant and go around to the back where David parks and turns off the engine, both the Dove and I letting out sighs of relief.

"Good friend," I say, jumping off, loosening the strap to my helmet, patting the seat. "Stood up to him. Didn't let him kill us all."

David eyes me sidelong, addresses the bike with a little pat as well. "Don't let her come between us."

I detect now something more than just facetiousness in his voice.

When I get back from the rest room, David has found us a table within view of the Dove.

"You always ride like that?" I say, laying into him the moment I'm seated.

"The guy sped up and cut me off," David says contritely. "You can depend on the Dove, Ma."

"I'm not depending on the Dove, I'm depending on you. Your father always said, 'The lane you're in is the best lane.' Why the hurry?"

"Look, we have a long way to go. I know what the Dove can do; you might trust her, and me, a little more if you understood her a little better. First lesson: the Dove is a 1975 BMW R75/6. You should know, if anyone asks. It's one of the safest and most reliable cycles on the road: its design makes it light and responsive for a good rider but forgiving of a poor one. It has a low center of gravity, with the balance and stability of a much heavier machine due to the engine's gyroscopic forces. And those cylinders sticking out—they protect the rider as well. I've done some modifications to make her go faster, stop quicker, and handle better, and she's never failed me, not in 100,000 miles."

"Save me, please!" I say, waving my hand to a passing waitress, who stops at our table. She is dark-haired, and pretty, and young. Youth by itself is pretty. I can see that she finds David handsome in his leathers. He flirts with her. "You look like the only flower in the desert," he compliments her, lamely.

She falls for it. Blushing, she takes his order first. After she leaves, a little smile of self-satisfaction on her face, David yawns.

"You're tired," I say, unable to stop myself, now that I've gotten started. "You knew we had to get up early. Do you have any idea how worried I was, picturing you out there on the Hollywood Freeway at 3:00 A.M., probably stopping without a second thought to help anyone whose car has broken down, stepping right into some serial killer's trap?"

"Why did you call Ben and Frank after midnight?" His tone is icy.

"How did you know that?"

"They called me this morning."

"So that's what's been bothering you."

"What do you mean 'that's what's been bothering' me?"

"You could have called, instead of letting me worry myself sick. They had no right to keep you that late."

"No right?"

"Why didn't they just ask you to stay over?"

"They're not responsible for me."

"You're the one who's not responsible!" I shout at him.

His eyes blaze now. (He's never looked so handsome, and I hate him for it.) "I can't just live according to your specifications. I can't pick out my life with one finger on the piano the way you'd like."

"I don't understand."

"What don't you understand?"

"You," I say now in a low voice, then almost as if I were talking to myself, "what's happened? I was so happy this morning. Why do I get along so much better with Mark? Is it some law of nature? Is it because I breast-fed him and I didn't you? Because it's too late now."

I fall silent as the waitress returns with our food. "We'd better eat," David says, sounding guilty.

I take one bite and put down my fork. I can't eat; my

stomach is churning. David too stops eating, pays the check, and leaves a generous tip. The waitress watches him as we leave—David oblivious, but I see.

In pain shall ye bring forth children. And forever after live in pain.

If only Leo were here to laugh at me, to call me Sarah Heartburn.

Back on the road it's cool now, and there is only the purring sound of the Dove.

After a while we pull off the road. The sun is setting. The desert is a huge glowing ruby, and except for the trill of a wren, seamlessly silent, as if it has stopped to take a deep breath.

David lifts his helmet and turns around. "Ma, you've suffered through the desert's bad moods. See how lovely it can be in a good mood."

Have we passed the hurdle? Is our quarrel ended? A sudden warmth for him wells up in me.

"The desert has a beauty of its own," he continues. "It's full of life. It wears a coat of many colors. If you look carefully, you'll see more than sagebrush and cacti. There are the flowers—pinks, yellows, purples, even lipstick-red redbuds. I've been in the desert at night, seen jackrabbit, hares, wild burros, bighorn sheep."

There follows a wild chorus of coyotes, barking and yelping out on the mountains. In the distance, a tall thin man rides a tall horse, making the desert seem lonely. But this too seems fitting. This is the desert, both good and evil, like our relationship. At this moment we share its strange beauty, and it brings us closer.

We are back on the highway. Past dark, the road runs black before us. The small yellow reflectors glow dimly under the headlight. I squeeze my eyes shut and open them onto a crimson night. Can I get used to this riding in the dark?

It is ten o'clock when we finally roll into Phoenix. The moon casts its silver-blue light over well-watered lawns and broad-limbed, pretty trees. We have arrived at Mark's apartment complex. He stands outside waiting, a big man with intensely blue, intensely worried eyes. Another worrier like me. How many times I have laughed at him, the psychologist: *Physician, heal thyself.*

But good old Mark and his breezy wit: he can always make everything all right. The huskier of the two, he kisses me, then lifts David and carries him across the threshold. The men hug, kiss, slap each other around, banter in Russian. Mark is the older by five years. He learned Russian at Stuyvesant High, New York, and began teaching it to his baby brother, accomplishing his goal: I could not understand them.

It is so rare to see them together. My eyes are wet. There's not much resemblance between my sons, except for the heavy brow, the cast of the eyes that suggest the same bloodlines, eyes expressive as weather reports.

I follow them into the bedroom: a mess of books, magazines, school papers. Mark hands David a plastic puzzle.

"Here you go, see how long it takes you to work this."

David smiles quizzically and works it out almost instantly.

Mark appears chagrined. He says to me, "My students still haven't figured it out." Then he adds, "Christine is coming over to meet you. You'll like her. She's a fairy tale."

I have just finished washing up and putting on my lipstick when she arrives. Mark barely has time to say, "Chris, this is my mother," before she kisses me!

"I love you, Mark's mother," she says. It's a bit gushy, but I like it, kissing her back. She is fair-skinned, with opaque-brown eyes, and thick bangs that lie like a branch of pine across her forehead. I have left a smudge of lipstick on her cheek.

"You're a doll," I tell her, daubing it away.

"I agree," says David.

"Doesn't she look like you, Ma?"

"Give her another thirty years, Mark."

After she leaves for work, David says, "If you don't marry her, I will."

"I'm considering it—that is, if she'll have me."

It is the first time ever that he's mentioned marriage.

"I wish I could find a woman who loves the land as Mom and I do," says David, his voice laced with sadness. "Someone like Christine…"

"Or Rachel?" I ask.

"Or Rachel," he says wistfully.

Mark and I look at each other. After she left, we know he did the primal scream thing up there on the mountain, with only the birds to accompany him. He had been married once before to a girl from a sunshine-warmed home in California, who found it too hard to live on that isolated mountain in the old, frostbitten shack where he spent the years before he built his house, with his chilblained fingers and a back turned arthritic.

"You're supporting a couple of foster children, aren't you?" Mark asks David.

"Right. I'm supposed to remember to send them post-cards."

Mark's dimples are showing. "Now that I'm a full professor, I'm rich enough to take one on myself. By the way, what have you heard from Rachel?"

"Hasn't answered the last letter I sent months ago," David says, matter-of-factly. "Maybe she'll call me at the rally. I sent her Michael's phone number."

Michael is a fellow cyclist. Rachel was a tenant in the tiny bungalow on David's land. She moved away when Barbie the Despicable moved in with David two summers ago. "He doesn't know I exist," Rachel told me, before she left for South Africa to teach English.

In time, Barbie went her usual transient way, too late for David to acknowledge that the attraction between Rachel and himself had been mutual. He wrote her, and for a while she replied. It usually took him months to answer her letters. And then nothing, their correspondence ceased.

"How do you feel about that?" Mark asks David.

"He feels lousy," I answer for him.

"David?" Mark gently prompts.

"Ask Mom. She knows how I feel about everything."

"I'm asking you."

"Lousy."

"That makes two of us," I have to chip in, doing it again.

At this point we need to nix the nostalgia. I show my sons how I can touch the floor with my full palms. David shows us the yoga exercise "Salute to the Sun." This small amount of exercise makes me realize how tired I am, although I am much too excited to sleep.

"Come on, I'll take you both out for coffee," Mark offers.

"Tea. Herbal tea," David corrects him.

"Iced for me," says Mark.

"Coffee for me," I say daringly.

"You won't be able to sleep, Ma," Mark warns.

"You have herbal tea too," David tells me firmly.

In the backseat so the men can sit together in front, I marvel at how comfortable it is to be in a car—not exciting, but comfortable. Mark drives solidly, as if he were an auxiliary part of the machine.

"Is Christine one of your students?" David asks.

"I don't date students. The ethical rigors of academia, remember?"

"David would," I say. "He's addicted to love." David's humorless silence announces, faux pas. "I'm sorry, I shouldn't have said that," I tell him.

His face softens at this rare apology. "I've been telling Ma she ought to move up to British Columbia. I think she belongs there."

Mark smiles. "She needs her own toilet."

"I'll build her her own outhouse," David offers.

We all laugh. David can make the idea of living near him so appealing: "In the winter, Ma, I'll tie a pair of skis on you. You can ski to the stream. There'll be sled rides and sleigh bells and moonlit nights when the snow's like talcum powder. And I could get you a horse. Your own. An oldie but a goodie."

Oldie but goodie? Like me, I think. But to be close to him, to live in his jeweled atmosphere is a dream I've given up on. I know what it's like to live with David and not feel welcome in his home. The old anger awakens, and with it the banging of my heart. Overwhelmed by the memory, my hands tremble now as they did two years ago.

We reach the neon-lit coffee shop. It's pretty around here, and quiet, not menacing like Los Angeles after dark. We are seated at the round table Mark uses when he meets here with his students. Our waitress is middle-aged and pleasant. She wears a long gingham dress, like all the waitresses. An old polished sideboard of mahogany-red wood holds Chinese dishes patterned with landscapes. Mark orders herbal teas all around, a large fruit salad for us to share.

To put all bad thoughts out of my head, I start cranking out the good memories. "David, do you remember when we went to Florida for the Christmas holiday? Oh, you wouldn't remember, you were so young."

"No, I do remember. It was wonderful. We clapped hands, sang 'Jimmy Crack Corn' and a whole bunch of other songs."

"That's right. Your father had called from work at five that afternoon. He said, 'How would you like to take a ride tonight to Florida?' As we talked, I remember watching from the window a nearly bodiless rain; the streets seemed almost depressed beneath the drizzle. 'I'm already half-packed,' I told him."

For those days, we were quite an unconventional family. The boys called their father "Leo" and were encouraged to do so. Leo liked it. I believe he felt it brought them closer to him, in a spirit of camaraderie. He had never felt close to his own father.

"You and Leo were two of a kind," Mark says. "I've never experienced that."

"Neither have I," confesses David, wistfully.

My heart aches for them both.

Now David has to ask, as he has so many times before, "When are you going to leave smog-bound L.A. and move where the air is clean? Even the birds there get emphysema."

"When are you going to stop taking these long journeys?" I counter. "God's getting pretty bored with my prayers for your safety."

David stops drinking and looks over his cup, angry. "I'd hoped you'd get as hooked on riding as I am."

I object to his tone. "Dammit, I didn't mean I'm not enjoying the trip, David. It's just that I feel like I have to protect you."

"Ma's your guardian angel, David," says Mark.

David is not reassured. "I wish she'd stop trying to control my life."

Now I let loose. "You know I can't live up there with you, but you keep asking. I know what's on your mind, that business with that … Barbie! You never noticed how she treated me—or you simply didn't care."

My blood is coursing now like wild wind on a forest fire. David's face has gone white, then red. "I never saw Barbie do anything mean to you. You just never gave her a chance. She always brought the things you needed down to the bungalow. It was you who never showed any gratitude!"

Then I'm shouting, "Are you out of your senses? Oh sure, you pretend to speak no evil, except of me!" I'm almost choking now, my heart is skipping beats. "So what's the point? What's the use of trying to get along with you?"

"You never like my friends."

"And you hate me for it! I can't do anything right."

We are both on our feet by now, stiff in our coats of emotional armor. And both in tears. Mark's face has paled. "Come on," I say to him, "let's get out of here."

"Both of you, sit down," he commands. His voice is stern, as if he were addressing two small children. "We're not going anywhere."

When we're reseated, David says, "I don't hate you. I love you, Ma," tears streaming down his face.

I have not seen him cry since Leo died.

Mark motions to the waitress to bring more tea. I cannot trust myself to speak. David too has fallen silent. We blink through the tears at each other. Mark hands each of us a napkin. I know how our anger hurts him. I look at the fruit salad and attempt a sorry little joke. "Eat up. Children are starving in India."

There is a smell of bacon burning, and outside a siren's screech makes me grit my teeth. David picks up a lemon peel and begins chewing on it.

If a plant can't live according to its own nature, it dies, and so a man.

Oh God, I wonder to myself, will we never understand each other?

Just before we get up to leave, Mark asks David, "Do you remember that small room with the bunk beds, and the noisy fish tank, the colorful guppies, the white mouse you kept in the cage? We had plenty of fun. Not all of it was clean fun."

A small, reluctant smile appears on David's face.

"That room always smelled like spit," I add, "like you boys had been urinating on the walls."

David and I are looking at each other now, eyes locked, remembering the way things used to be. Slowly he reaches out and places his hand over mine. "You really think I hate you? I wouldn't have asked you to come if I didn't love you. I really do want us to be close."

"David," I say, "do you have any idea how much you hurt me when you don't believe me? Remember when I told you that your friend Don sent me a postcard, and you said, 'Why would he write to you?', and I said, 'Because he wants to stay in *my* house while we're away,' and you said, 'Show me the postcard,' as if I'd lied."

And now I am crying again.

Mark quietly reminds him, "David, Mom doesn't lie."

David's hand tightens on mine; there is a huskiness in his

usually clear voice. "Believe me, Ma, I love you. I really do."

Two sons have I, two different mothers have my sons. There is love between David and me, but not of the calm, understanding variety that I enjoy with Mark. David's anger is my anger, his strong emotions are also mine. Times when our anger spouts up, I have the strange sensation that I am fighting myself. A few chosen words, however, can turn my anger away. Mark knows those words.

Back at Mark's apartment I am sleepy, thanks to the herbal tea. I go to bed and dream my recurring dream, the one I have had all my life, with Leo and since: I am running through a long corridor, looking for him, and I run out into the garden, where a ghastly moon is shedding milky-green light over the hedges. But he is nowhere to be found.

When I woke to find him at my side, I would hug him. He never knew why he got so many hugs at dawn.

That night, a clap and guttural growl of thunder wakes me as it runs through the apartment, rattling the windows. An exciting novelty: it rarely storms in Phoenix. The force of the fickle storm makes me keenly alert in every nerve ending. Secure in my room, the storm exhilarates me now. But how will I feel tomorrow when we are back on the road?

SUNDAY, JULY 8, PHOENIX, AZ

Our departure is postponed as the rain will continue into the day.

I have asked Mark to turn off the old air conditioner; the heat is preferable to the noise. Mark makes us a quick brunch of spaghetti and salad. We play Scrabble and I come in last. I'm thankful for this blessing of rain that has brought us together. Time now to talk, and so much to talk about, I'm feeling happy. The afternoon flies by and soon it grows dark.

That evening I invite my sons out for dinner. "My treat. Just to make you glad I'm alive."

Back in the car, this time we are going to a local Chinese restaurant. The storm has subsided. The streets appear scrubbed down and cool beneath the reflected light of the street lamps.

Inside the restaurant, I sit opposite them and watch the candlelight flickering on their faces: my sky, my earth, my sons. "In olden days, after the fast of Yom Kippur," I tell them, "the lines outside the Chinese restaurants in Brooklyn were so long we'd have to wait half an hour to be seated. I can't say my generation was particularly orthodox. That was before you were born, of course."

David looks at me earnestly. "I was an accident, Ma."

I am going to say, 'No, my darling, you were not,' but instead I say, somewhat irrelevantly, "I was just thinking what a pleasure it will be to get to know you."

Mark grasps, squeezes his brother's arm affectionately. "Everybody wants to get to know David."

Granted, but has David ever really gotten to know David? I wonder.

The diminutive waitress pads up to our table, bringing

our order of crisp Chinese chicken salad and egg fu yung, a pot of tea, and fortune cookies. David's turns out to be the most apropos: "Flee fornication." We laugh heartily enough to cause the other patrons to turn and look at us.

After dinner, Mark starts in on me, predictably. "You really ought to get out more often, meet some nice men. There must be someone you'd like. Haven't you been alone long enough?"

David touches my hand. "Mom's not alone."

I answer him anyway. "Mark, I want a man like your father, one with intelligence and humor. I want a marvelous man."

Always in a hurry, David takes this as his cue. "Come on, let's go, my marvelous mother. We need to get an early start." He picks up the check. I snatch it from him. He shrugs. "It doesn't matter, Ma."

"Yes, it does," I snap.

Easygoing David. Sometimes too easygoing.

As we pass the smoking section, a young man with shoulder-length hair gives me an unsanitary look and snickers.

"Did you see the way he looked at me?"

"The guy's a jerk," David assures me.

That soiled face, like a shadow falling across my path—I can't help feeling piqued. He is the whole callous young world out there, wounding with impunity. I should practice returning blow for blow, wound for wound. I understand now why I'm beginning to like being under the helmet: I'm free, I'm daring, I'm hopeful, even when its cumbersomeness is an irritation.

Back at Mark's apartment building, the rain splashes in great drops into the pool. In the crowded parking lot stands the Dove beneath its raincoat.

At the apartment, the rain has pushed long fingers under Mark's door. He places a towel on the floor at the entrance. We kiss each other good night and I go to bed. So early in the trip and I'm already so tired. If the rain continues, it will be a long hard day tomorrow.

Monday, July 9, Albuquerque, NM

In the morning the rain is still coming down in buckets. David makes us breakfast from our provisions. I am depressed enough at the thought of leaving Mark. Then David announces casually, "I'm planning to stop in Albuquerque, Ma."

Why Albuquerque? I wonder. Then it occurs to me... My scalp begins to tingle, my temples throb. "I know why. You want to see your very good friend Don. You said he was staying near Albuquerque, right? I bet he won't put us up, and we'll be out looking for campgrounds in the dark and rain. Why don't we just stay here another day? Riding in the rain is no fun."

"We can handle it," David insists, obstinately I think. "We have a deadline to meet, Ma. And besides, I just want to see him."

"You'll see him all right. He'll be visiting you soon enough for another six months. And never contribute a cent for food," I remind him.

"He'll get married and settle down one of these days."

"Really? That costs money, David. Better tie a stone around his neck and drop him in the ocean. That'll settle him down."

Something in me now says, *Shut up, you've said enough.* But I cannot help myself. "I don't understand. With me, you assert yourself. Why not him? David, it must have bothered you. You knew he was getting money in the mail from all his rental properties."

"Karma, Ma. What goes around comes around."

"Spoken like a true choirboy. David, will you never learn that half the world is out to screw the other half?" I have this compulsion to keep on talking. "Remember, last year when Mark set up the course for you, the self-awareness training—"

"When the hotel clerk wondered what the three of us were doing in one room."

I wave him away. It's not like David to interrupt. "I told Mark everybody would fall in love with you, and you'd emerge the same old self-unaware David."

"Look who's calling the kettle black, Ma," David says softly.

I appeal to Mark. "You're the psychologist, talk to him. A sane person can't deal with him."

Mark raises his eyebrows. "I don't like being caught between the two people I love most," he pleads.

I know I'm being unfair to him. It's Mark I'm hurting now. My good intentions are like old cloth: roughly handled, easily torn. Self-reproach finally silences me.

Watching David pack with quick, quiet efficiency, I feel again something of the thrill at the outset of our trip, at the promise of all its uncertainties. I really don't want to spoil it. Better that I learn tolerance now, I tell myself, learn to keep my mouth shut.

Still, I can't help whining later, "If only it would stop raining..."

David adjusts the helmet on my head. "You need to make the strap real tight," he tells me, pulling it tighter than I can. "When we get to the rally, maybe we can find a helmet more your size."

Just before we leave, Mark presses a bag of fruit on us. Then come the hugs and kisses. There is the electric smell of worry about him. My promise to phone him along the way is followed by more hugs and kisses. Mark tells David, "You'll be going through some beautiful country. Give Mom a chance to enjoy the scenery?"

His way of asking David to slow down. I don't look back as we zoom off.

The wind speed must be 40 mph, the rain pelts down furiously, the sky looks like beer going flat. My head knocks about in the damnably ill fitting helmet. The noise of storm and traffic is deafening. Half my friends don't hear well as it is; I don't need this, to boot.

Even the ordinarily cooing engine of the Dove seems to

be gasping for air. And here we are, braving hell and rising water just to see a man who to me is like a stiff whiff of halitosis.

Aging, getting on in years is like this: flawed, dusty, full of cracks. And yes, bitchy. Sometimes very bitchy.

Past Gallup, New Mexico, we stop by a lonely field abundant with cholla cactus. After an hour-long intermission, the rain is once again driving down, stinging my face like sand pitting glass. "I'm shivering," I tell David through clenched teeth. On the roof of a wet breeze, we have anticipated more bad weather and made a brief stop in Gallup, where David has bought us twin yellow rain suits at an army and navy surplus store.

Now he is helping me into my suit before putting on his own. When I bend down, I accidentally touch a cactus. It punctures the palm of my hand and I cry out. The pain is cruel.

David's voice is full of concern. "I'll take care of it, Ma." He helps me get my arms into the suit before he looks at the wound. From the fairing pocket he removes iodine, towelettes, adhesive bandages; carefully cleans the wound with a towelette and applies iodine, then a bandage. "It'll hurt for a while," he tells me.

Despite the pain, I am feeling warm and comfortable now. The rain suit makes all the difference. David studies the map, tracing the squiggly lines with an index finger. "Those are mountains. There'll be lots of them as we ride north."

Ominous sounds in my ears—I wave them away. There will be lots of mosquitoes as well.

The Dove stands wheel-rims-deep in mud. As we climb back on, I sing out, "Two canaries flown the coop!"

David turns his head and asks, "How's the hand?"

"I think it feels better already," I lie.

"Good." He races the bike's engine to free us from the mud. Soon, she is gracefully running back down the road.

All this space and sparseness and utter simplicity are amazing to one born and raised in the big city. It takes me back: ten weeks every summer at Mary's place in the mountains, rain and shine, Mary standing in front of the old farmhouse, arms folded, her Polish-blue eyes aglow in her frank face warm with dignity, ready to hold her arms out to the children who grew up loving her.

Seven families we were, who took over, besieged the farmhouse. Dressed in shorts, bandannas, we women teemed in that huge kitchen, sharing refrigerators, each cooking on her own range, glad to be away from the tenements and the noise and the foul air, missing our men, but taking pleasure in the anticipation of their weekend visits.

Once a week, with the help of the children, we picked and sucked the delicious warm round berries. They became pies bubbling in the ovens on Friday afternoons.

Early Friday evening, Leo would arrive climbing the hill in our newly acquired old car, playing "London Bridge" on the horn. David would run from the aluminum tub, naked and wet, jumping into his father's arms, laughing and hugging. All weekend, he would chase his father around, stumbling on his short feet, ride head held high on his father's shoulders. Whose heart didn't beat faster on such days! When his father left, a teary David ran to hide.

Of course, the weekends included what Mark Twain called "the sex refreshments" and afterward the women all teasing each other.

So long ago and yet so vivid. I think about the way a single event can forever divide a life into the Before and After.

I have grown drowsy. My helmet must have been hitting David's back because he is poking me awake. We are in Albuquerque and suddenly I remember. I had happily forgotten about our rendezvous with Don.

On the far side of town we come to a muddy, bumpy road and turning up it, almost veer into a ditch. Don stands outside the isolated farmhouse. He greets us with a mouthful of prominent yellow teeth.

"This is the home of some friends," he notifies us right off the bat, showing us inside. David had given me the impression we would be visiting one of Don's rental properties. Don says, "Sorry I can't offer you dinner. The food's all theirs."

"That's all right," David says. "We have food with us. Will we be able to sleep over? We have sleeping bags. We could sleep right here on the floor."

I have noticed there is an enclosed porch that our host fails to show us.

"Well..." says Don, pausing to unwrap a piece of gum

and stick it in his toothy mouth, "I think it'll be okay. I'm not sure. They may come back tonight," he warns, chewing the gum.

Six months this man lived in David's home as a guest. I do not like his white-rat look, his pale eyes, pale hair.

"Look, if the sun comes out, then we'll leave," David assures him. "We have a long way to go, anyway."

By now I am thoroughly disgusted. "I think we should go now," I suggest.

"We just came," David says.

End of discussion, everybody seems to be at the brink of a hem or haw. We all sit down. To break the ice, I tell David I am enjoying the Vonnegut and Stephen King books he brought along. Every book we discuss Don says he has read, "but it was so long ago, I forget it. I went to M.I.T.," he informs me.

What, was he a janitor there?, I am tempted to ask him. I would like to see his diploma. Very lucky for him that his father left him a lot of property. "If the women knew how much money I have, I'd be as popular as David," he once boasted to me.

He tells David now, "I spent only five hundred dollars in the last six months. I have this idea, to save money on my tax return…"

As he explains, he preens himself over his iota of brilliance. I smile sweetly at him when he finishes. "You may need a criminal lawyer to help you fill your return out." I keep looking out the window at the depressing rain coming down like sheets of aluminum foil. Finally I say to

David emphatically, "Let's go."

"Ma, it's awful out there."

"You didn't seem to mind this morning."

"Look, if Don's friends do come back, I'm sure they won't mind our sleeping on the porch."

I am adamant, as only I can be. The thunder inside me drowns out any rumblings outdoors. "I want to go, David. Now."

Don says nothing to dissuade us. Instead he says, "I'm thinking of moving to Los Angeles, buying a house." He is watching me for my reaction.

"How nice!" I exclaim sourly. "I'll be sure to notify the L.A. Welcome Wagon." Then I say what I have been waiting to say. "Thank you for the postcard."

In response, Don mumbles something I can't make out, but David hears. He says as he rises abruptly, "Well, I hope to see you soon."

Back on the trail, for a few minutes we ride under clear skies. Desert thunderstorms, I'm learning, are hit-and-run affairs. This allows David the opportunity to turn on the intercom, which can only be used in good weather.

"Roger, can you hear me? Over."

"Yes, I can hear you. Who's Roger?"

"I know you're hungry. Can you hold out until we get to Santa Fe? It'll be about an hour."

"Your friend is a crumb," I answer instead. "It's obvious he didn't want us around."

The intercom goes dead.

Why do I bother to fight him? I confess it, I don't have the patience of Job. I cut off communications like a raging gale felling telephone lines. I have my prejudices, my peeves. My dislikes are as passionate as my likes.

Still, I am trying to puzzle out this enigmatic son of mine, how he could possibly tolerate someone like Don. I conclude he must feel sorry for this pathetic man who, his net worth aside, is otherwise impoverished, trapped in a small mind.

A rainbow arches across the ruddy sky. Just ahead looms some hellish rain and the onset of darkness. Suddenly a bolt of lightning throws the trees in a field along the highway into brilliant relief; just as quickly the sky and road blacken again to a sheer ebony. The lightning has frightened me. I imagine us riding over a cliff, dashed to a broken, bloody mess. Every tendon in my toes tenses up, my thighs stiffen. This is David's barometer. He will know now that I am afraid.

A darkened bus ahead, the driver takes it very slowly, no sign of life inside, as if it were a mobile morgue. If I could see inside, I could fantasize about the faces, their lives, a favorite game of mine when I travel.

David whizzes past the bus. Then we pass an already speeding pickup. This makes me angry again, and again I pummel David's back with my fists. He pulls off the road and comes to a skidding halt.

"Why did you do that?" he demands.

"You just had to pass that truck, didn't you?" I yell at him.

"I haven't done anything wrong!" he yells back, then calms down. "Ma, do you realize the stress you put me under? What if you got sick again and there were no rest areas around? You know, we could have avoided this, if it weren't for your stubborn pride! So what if Don didn't want us? He would have put us up and shut up. He owes me that."

Back on the road I am feeling chastened, remorseful. But at least David did say, "He *owes* me that," which is some kind of acknowledgment of the existence of mutual obligation, a quid pro quo, which, coming from David, is a huge acknowledgment.

My scarf flutters out of my pocket and again I feel the terrible uncertainties of the fury of the wind, the thunder growling, the lightning flashing: *Life is precarious, I spare you for now, but be forewarned.* Even the Dove seems to shiver, but holds the road.

David reminds me that the Dove can go thousands of miles without a breakdown, but that's hard for me to believe. Every trip Leo and I made, our car broke down. We never owned a new car.

Drenching dark, no moon or stars. The narrow beam of the headlight hardly penetrates the pitch-blackness all around us. Can David really see any better than I? We might as well be rolling through the bowels of the underworld. I am practically dizzy with fear.

At first I believe the lights in the distance must be a mirage, but they're really Santa Fe. It looks as if we may survive this leg of our trip after all. I really hadn't been sure at all there for a while, but now I am like a little girl again laughing on a lit-up merry-go-round, and Papa is catching the brass rings, a free ride for each one.

It must be at least ten o'clock when we sweep into town. We pull up at the first motel we see. Helmets in hand, we walk into the office. The quoted rate is exorbitant. Looking at our helmets, the manager says, "There are cheaper places, but they're all booked up. You'll be back."

David and I look at each other. A few more such lodgings and we will be walking to the rally. "We'll take it," he says.

Under cascading rainfall now, David moves the Dove to the door of our room and begins to unpack her, bringing in as much as he can carry. I bring along the suitcase. The room is warm and comfortable enough.

"We shouldn't have walked in with our helmets," I say.

"It's only money. We'll survive." These are the exact words his father used in our many financial dilemmas.

I want to help him bring in the rest of our things, but he insists I stay in the room and out of the rain. While he fits the Dove with its rain cover, I take a quick shower and get into my blue flannel nightgown. David returns with the kit'n'kaboodle, even the sheepskin seat cover I sit on. "Aren't you hungry?" he asks. "We haven't eaten."

"Who cares," I say. I lie across the bed, dry and comfortable. I have left the bed by the window for David so he can see the Dove.

"You know, he'll be visiting you for another six months," I have to repeat. "And he didn't even offer us a drink."

"Ma," David sighs patiently, "you've taught me to be

decent and kind, to care about people."

"I didn't teach you to be a fool."

Or did I?

Suddenly it occurs to me how much I have changed over the years. Didn't my mother used to speak to me this way? I have grown so much more suspicious than in my more vulnerable youth, when I couldn't bear to give offense. Then, when people did things I found reprehensible, things that made me ashamed of them, I could never be honest and tell them so. Now I can't seem to shut up! Why must I do this? If David were to tell me to go home, I would. Pride still goes before a fall.

For him the subject has been exhausted. "Do you want to get dressed and go out?"

"At this hour, in this weather? No, thank you," I decline peevishly, close to tears. We sit quietly a while before I say, "I guess you'd like to send me home?"

"No," he replies gently.

I'm speechless, my heart lurching, tripping once more over his love.

TUESDAY, JULY 10, SANTA FE, NM

I found a note from Leo on the table one day years ago. *You know where we've gone. Love and kisses.* And under his father's name, David had added, *Me too, love and kisses.* Their handwriting was remarkably similar. They were constant companions, from the barber to the library. At the bowling alleys, David kept score while his father collected trophies.

After Leo's death, the house fell silent. No laughter, no music. I paid little attention to David's gloomy comings and goings; I never knew where he was or what he was doing, nor much cared. For me, it was natural that the music had ceased, but for him it was completely out of character, this grief and frustration.

He decided to go to Canada, to British Columbia. This I cared about: he had only a year and a half left to complete college. But for both our sakes, he had to go. Half relieved, I let him.

Later I sent him what was left of the insurance money: $4,947.23, to the penny. With all the debts since Leo's illness, there was not much left over. I sent it along with a letter. "Buy yourself a piece of land," I wrote him. "Don't let this melt in your hot little hands."

David bought that land, felled trees, began building a house in minus thirty-degree weather. That was when he earned his chilblained fingers and his arthritic back.

"Don't worry," he wrote me. "I'm fixing cars and toilets. My hands are good hands."

In the spring, he planted. "My carrots, cauliflower, and cabbage are coming up. I won't starve, Ma."

People in town began hearing about the young man living alone on the mountain with just his dog; heard about all his skills, his honesty in plying them, and began bringing their cars the eight miles up the mountain from town.

"I'm ashamed to pay him as little as he asks," the beautician in town told me.

How well liked he is in a town where—should I add?—he is the first Jew.

I love the unpretentious home he designed and built for himself: stained-glass windows, a central staircase winding gracefully to the second-floor loft, only two doors to the outside, but the inside all open, just as he is. I am filled with pride when I stand on his round stone steps, gazing at the sheltering pine above, the shimmering lakes below. Blueberries, raspberries, and strawberries grow wild and abundant. Birds find refuge here. Here the stars come out shining like giant opals.

The mostly classical music comes on even before he lights the fire. Just like his father, he loves music.

Living his solitary existence, sad at times in its isolation, but purposeful, pure as lake and primeval forest, he has proven himself. How much he has accomplished! And yet this is the son I rage at? I watch him breathing quietly and deeply as he sleeps.

When I woke this morning, my eyes, often inflamed by the Los Angeles smog, seemed to be on their way to healing. Still, I'm feeling blue. My rare fits of anger at his father always depressed me like this. But we were lovers. I used to wrap myself in the bedcovers and turn my back, but soon I would wake, cover him, give him a hug, and he would say, "Thank you, sweetheart."

It isn't so simple with my son. I badly want the intimacy, the soul talk between us, the barriers to come down. But instead I'm building a wall.

Morning filters in through the curtains. I rise from bed and open them just as David opens his eyes. The sky is the palest of blues, the air dry and weightless. It's a good day for a quest.

I bend down and kiss David's cheek. "Good morning."

He kisses me back. "Thank you, Ma."

The sun has struck a match to the grass, the trees, the pale chrysanthemums; its rays are like a creeping flame burning away at the edges of the low, whitewashed buildings. David has stopped, parking the Dove so that we can walk down the main drag. It is a comforting thought that here in Santa Fe, we will relax, eat, take a breather.

We stop to look at the Native American arts and crafts—rugs, pottery, ceramics, jewelry, traditional dress, dolls—displayed between two huge white columns. A young woman in a flashy blouse and silk pantaloons shows me a bronze bracelet. It is a lovely thing, etched with deities of some description. "We'll take it," David says, and pays for it. He clasps it around my wrist, where it lies sparkling in the sunlight.

"She looks like something out of *Arabian Nights*," David says of the shopkeeper when we are out of earshot.

"And she charges like the forty thieves," I add.

David is smiling. "It wasn't that much money. Besides, it was worth it to see your face light up like that. We'll worry about the money when we need to."

I look at the bracelet fondly. He's right. And I am feeling good about it.

Nice for a change not to be pelted by the rain, I think, as we amble along. There's a light breeze. It's eleven o'clock when we enter a Mexican restaurant. The waitress, a tiny Hispanic girl in a black-and-red miniskirt, is smiling to herself as if she is still basking in last night's afterglow. I order a chile relleno and a burrito. David orders a tostada, refried beans, and rice. The food is exquisitely well pre-pared, delicately spiced. Worth a trip back, if I'm ever invited again.

WEDNESDAY, JULY 11, COLORADO ROCKIES

Colorado-bound, we have made a pit stop in Taos. This is Pueblo Indian territory, a sunny, pastel-colored town pop-ulated with handsome people of varied descent, from Spanish to Native American. We have stopped at the post office, where David buys postcards. We have refueled the Dove.

The day is cool and clear, a brief lull in the series of storms. We sit on a bench under a mesquite tree, writing cards. David drops his cards and mine to Mark into a mail-box, and we're off again. David's excitement is quickening.

Up we go, beginning the first of our ascents to the high mountain passes of Colorado, two narrow lanes. The wind is rising. David gestures at the extravagant beauty of the "grandscape." The drop off the highway shoulder has become sheer. I am terrified that he may veer off in the same direction he's pointing. *You drive, I'll look,* I want to tell him. He calls it "scenic"; I equate that with "dangerous."

Above the timberline, we encounter wildflowers, sparse grass, ribbons of lingering snow garlanding the mountain peaks above.

David stops to take photos. I pull off the confining helmet and break one of my gold earrings. Not ordinary gold earrings, these have a history:

For ten years I had an ongoing correspondence with an American professor—"an overseas junkie," as a friend of mine describes the type—who was teaching in Saudi Arabia. A parcel of my poems had somehow reached this Saudi university in error. Dr. Bill rescued them, read them, and sent me a letter of high praise. I responded with trunk loads of poetry. Soon we discarded formalities, addressed each other by first name, and closed our letters with "Love." Our friendship was like Keats's Grecian urn, something permanent in a world of change. And like me, Bill was a Pisces. "Pisces should marry Pisces," he wrote.

The earrings were a gift from him. They bear the royal seal of Saudi Arabia. Every now and then some Saudi recognizes it.

My reverie is interrupted by a sudden veering of the Dove. David has narrowly missed killing some small animal. He would never forgive himself if he killed even the lowliest of creatures.

But in sum, Bill and I were poor fish, destined never to meet. We lost contact. My last letter came back stamped *Address Unknown.*

We are expected at Connie and Jim's in Colorado Springs tomorrow, where we plan to spend at least two nights enjoying much-needed sweet, sweet sleep in real beds.

I have met Jim three times before: twice at my home in California and another time in Canada, with his wife, Connie, about whom the chief thing I remember is the way she claimed drinking coffee made her breasts lumpy. For weeks after, I would examine my own after every caffeine break.

David says they have two boys now. I worry about the schlep-along situation I'm in and wonder whether I'll be welcome.

Our goal for tonight was a town called Walsenburg, but because we left Santa Fe late, we won't make it there till tomorrow. We never intend it, but we always seem to put in when it's already dark. And we'll be sleeping out tonight.

We're due to arrive at the rally July 19, perhaps even sooner. I'm dreading it—the crowds of boisterous bikers, my decrepitude sticking out in the midst of so much youth—but I hide this fact from David, who talks like we're cruising toward Paradise.

The weather has turned threatening again. The sky is scalloped with thunderheads; the wind has become biting. We stop at a supermarket. Since his teenage years, David has been trying to teach me how to interpret food labels. Inhaling the smell of barbecued chicken makes me salivate. I dutifully follow him around the store as he does the buying: Kretschmer wheat germ, peaches, sourdough bread, bananas, and cheese. No chicken.

Back at the Dove, David wets a chamois cloth and wraps

the perishables, placing them in the bike's left fairing pocket where they will stay cool and fresh.

We seat ourselves at a picnic table outside the market. David sets out a red paper tablecloth, silverware, the two carved wooden plates thoughtfully wrapped up in moist towelettes. We dine on tuna with pumpernickel, granola bars, and tomato juice. Very elegant.

Over the meal I tell him, "David, I worry about you. You're too daring. I'm always afraid you're in some physical danger."

He takes my concern well this time. "I worry about you too, Ma. You're too absentminded. I'm afraid you'll suck your thumb and jam it into a light socket."

I laugh. I can be a good sport when I'm just being joshed.

We ride on, looking for a campsite. And here comes the pain in my knee again. I stretch my foot off the foot peg. David takes note, stops at a wooded rest area where there is a bench, a table, and an outhouse. He massages my knee.

Whenever we go to a tragic movie, he is always the last one to rise, always with wet eyes. He's evasive about showing it, but a mother notices her son's tears.

We finally sight a campground, stop, and settle in. As usual, it's already dark. In the light of the wafer-thin, white disk of a moon, David washes our silver and dishes under a rusty faucet, then hangs the wash towel on the spike of a picket fence. There is only one other tent in view, near the rest rooms. The tree trunks and leaves appear in silhouette against the moonlit sky. The quiet of the night is punctuated by the sounds of the forest, the lapping of a nearby lake, an occasional birdcall.

I massage David's arthritic back. He reciprocates by clipping my toenails. I have painted them red for this trip, but the paint is already chipping. He massages my knee again. Should I request a back massage? I am unaccountably shy with this grown man who is also my son.

David starts by saying, "You know, my friends can't believe a woman of your age—"

"You tell your friends my age?" I interrupt, sharply. I don't think much of that.

"Why not? Ma, I'm proud of you! Always have been. When I was a little boy, I loved having you come to class."

"My age is nobody's business but mine. I consider asking my age a hostile question."

"You're just vain, Ma."

My anger subsides. In fact I am delighted with the turn of the conversation. "So what? Vanity has gotten me everywhere. Men used to call me 'Gypsy.' I liked that. You're right, I'm vain. Or I used to be."

The piney smell of the woods, the clear sense of peace, and the night that has turned out to be just right, with my youngest by my side—it reminds me of long-ago nights, the children bathed and in their beds, Leo and I in the living room reading together, the shelves lined with all Leo's books, my paintings on the paneled walls, a fire glowing in the hearth, strains of "Vienna Woods."

I remember sitting on the floor, my head resting against

Leo's knees, reading Simone de Beauvoir's *The Second Sex*. I remember it precisely because Leo had said that if he were a woman, he would certainly read it. I have an impossible longing to relive such nights, a yearning for that all's-right-with-the-world time of my life when I could look forward with desire to the good-night kiss, the fondling, the ensuing contentment and good physical exhaustion, the naive "bless you."

When did this ecstasy end? When the children grew older and my anxieties increased?

I know. It ended when Leo became ill and we could no longer laugh.

All my life I have been profligate with time and money, but my memories I hoard. Now I must come to terms with them and myself as I never have before. I must learn to put the regrets behind me. To drop them by the side of the road.

I am ready for a deep sleep. "David, I have to go to the rest room."

"Take the flashlight," he advises.

"Don't need to, the moon's so bright."

The path is silvery under the moonlight. As I head for the women's rest room, I stop dead in my tracks, appalled by the sight of a man walking stark naked in the same direction.

I'm breathless when I return to our campsite.

"What's the matter?" David asks, alarmed at first.

"I saw a naked man!"

"You never saw a naked man before?"

"He had an erection," I explain.

"You never saw a naked man with an erection before?"

"David, really now!"

His green eyes glint in the moonlight. "Was he going in or coming out?"

"Going in."

David throws back his head and laughs a throaty, lyrical laugh. "Ma, I'm sure he had no intention of molesting you."

Living in Los Angeles has done this to me. My morbid imagination always assures me that this man is a murderer, that man a rapist, or at the very least they're both muggers.

David quickly walks me back to the rest room and waits.

In the middle of the night the rain comes rattling in. I have to groan. David jumps up, brings in everything we have left outside, including the sheepskin, all except for the food in the fairing pocket. The edges of the tent are getting wet.

He places the suitcase in the middle of the tent, then he pays me a much needed compliment: "I promise you, this is the rainiest journey I've ever taken on the Dove. You're a good sport, Ma."

THURSDAY, JULY 12, COLORADO SPRINGS, CO

When we wake, it is still dark, and the rain is drenching. "David," I say, good sport or not, "if there's any place on the planet where it's not raining, let's go there."

David remains philosophical. "You might as well enjoy it, Ma. Take a deep breath, smell the good smells."

I take a deep breath and ask, "What day is it?"

"The twelfth. We should get to Colorado Springs tonight, and there'll be warm beds waiting for us."

He hands me a glass of juice and a granola bar, and reviews the itinerary: the stop in Walsenburg, then from there only ninety-one miles to Colorado Springs and Connie and Jim's.

Another day of speed, slick roads, and the fear I must hide. I remember how I once rode the Coney Island Cyclone three times, not out of fearlessness but out of fear; a fourth time would have been a bore.

I wonder if the mountain climber experiences the same thrill when he has reached his mountaintop. This weather seems to be my Kilimanjaro. The earth today does not smell sweet—good, but not sweet—but at least I will be sleeping in a bed tonight.

David's back is twitching. He is in pain. I massage his shoulders under the leather jacket as we ride into sunshine. He points out the rainbows. Again I want to say, *You do the steering, I'll do the sight-seeing.*

Almost in a fetal position, my helmet touching David's back, I must have dozed off again. David elbows me awake, begins massaging my knee. And when I have recovered my senses, I seem to really be seeing, for the very first time, the Colorado Rockies. They are achingly lovely, the very definition of "beautiful."

"To me, you'll always look like the first time I saw you: beautiful," Leo used to say to me on every anniversary. "Will it make you happy?" he was always asking me, with a smile and a wink.

Absentmindedly, I find myself singing "Stardust." Leo won first prize singing that song at the Brooklyn Loew's Pitkin, with its ceiling of stars. He dedicated it to "my girl." Proud and teary-eyed, I was that girl.

If only my sons could find such fulfillment.

Hazy sunshine now, and meadows, marshes, cornfields, rock-candy air. I would love to stop and take a nap, never mind the wet ground and carnivorous mosquitoes.

David has just switched on the intercom. "Ma, there's a scenic road that leads up to the alpine tundra. It's a detour, it'll take some extra time, but it's too beautiful to miss."

We climb, up, up the Continental Divide, two and a half miles. At the top I slide stiffly off the Dove. I'm hugging myself. "It's cold up here."

"No thermal underwear, Ma? I warned you."

In July?! I thought at the time. Ridiculous!

David has his camera out and is snapping pictures of the sights: far off, the deep blue of the sky cresting craggy peaks still frosted with snow; in the near distance, bright wild-flowers and patches of deep-green grass. David turns the camera on me.

"If you keep me here long enough, you'll get a picture of a glacier," I crack.

He points to the distance. "If we stand here long enough, we'll see a mountain goat on one of those cliffs."

The suggestion alarms me. "We're not really going to wait, are we?"

"No, Ma." He's laughing. "All those cliffs there were cut by glaciers during the Ice Age," he informs me. "Let's walk a little."

I am shivering now, but the cold invigorates me. I see some young boys and girls in shorts and wonder how they do it. A small boy points at us in our helmets and rain suits. "Look, Pa, men from Mars!" His father smiles at us and lifts the boy so that he can enjoy the view.

On the way back down the mountain, I ruminate on how I like cold better than heat.

Lower down we skirt a broad meadow, then come along a clear, cold, spring-fed stream where David stops to get us some water, using his long-handled tin cup. He offers me some.

"No, thank you," I tell him. "I'm still defrosting."

As we continue to descend, we ride through timberland with trees so tall one cannot see the tops, and yet only minutes ago we were above them.

Stopping in a small town off the highway, David checks the map but cannot find it. At the market he gases up the Dove, while I use the rest room and grab a paper cup of hot chocolate.

We head back out to the highway, almost reaching it before David suddenly changes direction and races back. Catching up with another motorcycle back at the market, we glide up next to them: it's David's friend Michael and his wife. "Am I glad to see you!" David says.

David has great respect for Michael, who is ten years his senior. A dedicated cyclist, Michael is one of the organizers of the rally. David asks Michael what's happening.

His reply is laconic and unsmiling. "Three casualties so far: one struck by lightning, one heart attack, another who apparently thought the road ran straight. Ran right into the trees. Killed instantly."

The west wind, full of bird cries / I never hear the west wind, but tears / Are in my eyes. David never mentioned there would be casualties.

Michael is an attractive man, a blend of John Wayne and Clark Gable. Not my type—I suspect he has too much hair on his belly. Michael's wife is a busty blonde. She says, "I'm not going again. Let him go alone. If I want to go anywhere, I'll take my camper. Anyway, we only fight when we're together."

I find her annoying. *Lady,* I want to ask her, *do you know what it is to be alone, year after year, to travel alone, no one to share in your experiences, fearing that your love life is prematurely over? What sort of future is that to look forward to?*

Love is a cathedral that takes many years to build. Nearing the end, Leo had said, "Who will love you as I did?"

My sons are my only future now. David has given me the opportunity to look beyond the gathering shadows, to raise my head, to look up and see the glorious, terrible stars from my perch on the Dove, where I watch my memories rising, floating to the surface of my consciousness, developing slowly, coming into sharper focus like photographic images materializing under the red light of a darkroom.

Michael's wife is still complaining: "And of course we've had nothing but rain."

Listening to her, my own nagging shames me. I have had neighbors like her, and I avoided them and their complaints about how hard they had to work to keep their houses clean, about their husbands, their laxatives, their horror stories of obstetrical calamities. I used to push my babies in their carriage far out of my way just to avoid them.

Michael now shrugs off his wife's kvetching and waves good-bye as David turns the Dove back toward the highway. Then we're off again, like a low-flying 747.

Nothing short of an act of God will stop us from getting to South Dakota on time.

Up on the Continental Divide once again, where the mountainsides have become a still life of buttercups, alpine forget-me-nots, and dwarf clover, David has stopped to take photos. The sky overhead has become thickly populated with birds making their lively music. I am told to keep looking for the blue columbine, Colorado's state flower, which we see at last in abundance on our way down.

Now the wind is sweeping across our path with terrific force. The sun has disappeared and the day has turned a sterling silver. The rain begins to fall in sporadic drops, like a man desperately trying to hold back tears. We pass the timberline and stop at another of those pure mountain streams. This time I drink the sweet water from the long-handled tin cup.

At the bottom of our descent, we make Colorado Springs. Connie and Jim's is just six miles away on the outskirts of town. But first we make a stop and look for a restaurant.

There is a sameness about these western towns, with their mingling aromas of Mexican food and charcoal-broiled steaks. I would opt for either. I am partial to sodium and cholesterol, especially when served up on white tablecloths with white linen napkins.

David again is the spoiler. "Smell all that grease? No way, Ma."

The rain now comes down in a weak drizzle, but I'm not cold anymore. We pass a high-steepled church, and, nearby, another, smaller one with cracked stained-glass windows, humble as a broken front tooth. The rain starts to come down more heavily now.

We walk past a movie house and come to a small market. Sans cholesterol, sans sodium, it's an uninteresting prospect, but it does offer a haven from the rain.

David holds the door open as people rush in. I stand behind him, trying to rush him in, but he continues to hold the door open until everyone else is through. "Thanks a lot, Sir Walter Raleigh," I say, wiping the rain from my eyes when we're finally inside.

"You could have gone in. You didn't have to wait behind me," he observes simply, letting me walk ahead.

"Just like you, letting everyone get ahead of you," I say.

I turn and his gaze falls on me like a blow. "I can't be rude. And speaking of rudeness, I wish you wouldn't interrupt people the way you do."

"Well, who in that line said 'thank you'?" I defend

myself. "They didn't even acknowledge the courtesy. And I'm the rude one?!"

There is a loud clap of thunder, and I think it must be coming from inside me. We stop and eye each other now like two bantam cocks. I'm trembling. "You're such a fool. You make me sick," I tell him.

There is a twitch in his left cheek I haven't seen before. The blood has drained from his face. He says nothing, walks on ahead of me, drops his helmet down on a bench in a booth next to the water fountain. I take the other bench before tearing my helmet off, with my head nearly still in it. "If you harbor such ugly thoughts about me, why did you ask me to come?" I ask him.

He looks at me and says with deadly calm, "Sometimes I wonder."

I look down at my shaking hands. My appetite is gone. I want to howl.

Then suddenly, in a conciliatory tone, he says, "Ma, I think what's wrong is that we're both hungry. If you don't mind waiting, I'll call Jim and Connie, tell them where we are, pick up some groceries for them."

Now I'm ashamed. "It's all right," I say.

"You can wash your hands in the fountain. I'll find out where the rest rooms are."

After he walks off, I sink down into the booth and put my head in my hands. He's right, of course. I have no patience with anyone.

I need a distraction. A tall, gaunt man enters with a thin, little woman wearing thick glasses. She has a nervous, fidgety manner. They are having an argument, apparently about money. I conclude they are sexually incompatible. Maybe I can amuse David with my observation.

Another clap of thunder causes me to convulse with a shiver. Struck by lightning—one of the casualties Michael mentioned. I dread these storms, mine and the heavens'. I try to relax. Only a few miles from safe haven now...

Soon David is back, grocery bags in both arms. He's smiling. "I told Jim you're with me. He said you're a fun person." I send Jim a silent thanks for supporting my cause. "Jim says you're not the everyday mother."

David is opening a can of tuna with his pocketknife. He looks at me and winks, *Let's forget the fight.*

"You look just like your father when you wink like that."

"Ma, I'm me. I wish you'd remember that. Besides, you might take responsibility for some of my traits you don't like."

"All right then, deny thy father. So what does that make you?"

It's a poor joke.

A week after Leo's death, David came home late one night and found me sitting on the kitchen floor in a pool of rising water, crying. The water heater had broken. He turned off the water, raised me to my feet, and helped me to bed.

"Ma, I'm not my dad," he reminded me before he covered me and kissed me good night.

I watch him now as he mashes an avocado into the tuna, adds slices of apple, and carefully folds the salad onto the seven-grain bread. Why must I always watch what I say to him? Mark and I understand each other so easily. But then I nursed Mark as a baby. It seems ridiculous, but I still sometimes wonder if that made a difference.

Why can't I hold my tongue? Is it really that difficult?

Before we eat, David reaches over and gently removes my dark glasses. I hadn't realized I was still wearing them. He washes them at the fountain and carefully dries them with a napkin. "How can you see through these things? You're not back in L.A. now. Here they'll just think you're depraved. I'll hold on to them for you."

He puts them in his breast pocket. He knows how I forget things—not people, not places, just things—how I spend half my domestic life on the hunt. Mark deals with my absentmindedness by saying, "Ma, we're playing that game again," and by helping me find what I'm looking for. But if I begin nagging him about something that happened a long time ago, he says, "See, Ma, you *do* have total recall," which makes us both laugh.

There is nothing wrong with David's sense of humor either—nothing but me.

I can tell by David's wary eyes he wants to tell me something, but he hesitates, and for once I anticipate and speak first. "David, I'm glad you called Jim. I'm always apprehensive about whether your friends want me around."

"There you go, feeling sorry for yourself. You contribute, in your own way."

My eyebrows go up. "Oh yeah, how's that?"

"By being outrageous sometimes. You can be fun."

"*You* don't always think so."

His face tightens. "That's true. Sometimes I don't."

"David, I try to live my life as simply and intelligently as I can. Didn't Einstein say something about that?"

David is smiling now. "Einstein speaks of the universe out there that exists independently of us, that doesn't need us. We take ourselves too seriously."

I like this. The detachment of abstract conversation makes me feel I am on safe, solid ground. I pick up a piece of lettuce and try to chew it, no longer a simple thing with these partials.

Then I remember there is someone in Colorado Springs I hope to avoid.

Drumming the table, I watch an elegant-looking woman pass. Dressed in a tight black dress, black designer hose, a broad-brimmed black hat trimmed with grosgrain, she seats herself in the booth where the thin couple were sitting. I am about to say to David, "There goes the TV siren Elvira," when I see her face. It startles, then saddens, me: pasty-white and lined, she is beyond the age when a face-lift could make any difference. She looks ready for her own funeral.

Many of the older people I know are still enjoying life and are not obviously consumed with a dread of aging.

"Do you remember the Barberas?" I ask David.

"Sure. Louise made the best lasagna."

"Louise is dead. I called to give my condolences to Carmen. He has to be the most foppish, fastidious man I've ever known: chesterfield coat, gold-headed cane, derby, and such royal manners. His daughter Catherine answered the phone. She said, 'He'll come to the phone, but he just crawls now. You know he's eighty years old.' Then she yelled at him, 'Chew your food first. And wipe your mouth!' Why is old age treated with such contempt, David?"

He puts on his helmet, picks up the groceries, and I follow him out. He packs the groceries, including two bottles of wine, into the traveling cases and pulls the straps tight. "Ma," he finally answers me, "I don't like general statements. That was a general statement."

David climbs onto the bike. I clamber up behind him—I can do this easily now, general statement or not—and we're off.

The Dove is shining its small light down the moonless road when I remember an old song, *"It's a long, long time from May to December..."* Why this tune?

Again I remember there is someone in Colorado Springs that I don't want to see, when suddenly, David swerves and I'm thrown back, coming briefly eyeball to frightened eyeball with a large, soft creature, only a heavy shadow in the night that just as suddenly vanishes.

Then I realize it was a deer! How David managed to avoid it is beyond me.

A biting rain is coming down again. I'm shuddering. My thighs tense, David's barometer. He rolls off the road to a stop. "You all right?" he asks.

"That was scary, but I'm all right."

"I had my moment there too," he confesses, smiling.

A car slows down, long enough for a man to shout out,

"Why don't you trade that thing in for a boat? *Deers* don't swim."

"The guy has no class," David says.

"No grammar either. He just can't appreciate what a bike like this can do. Well, he'll never get a ride from you."

"Who knows? That might change his mind."

David—tolerant of everyone. Or nearly everyone.

A suburb outside of Colorado Springs: the softly lit windows of the large houses overlook sprawling lawns shaded by great spreading trees. The night air is fragrant with the scent of fir. The Dove cruises smoothly down these wide, level streets. When we reach the iron gates of Connie and Jim O'Connor's home, a dog barks and the outside lights come on. Arriving on a motorcycle strikes me suddenly as a splendid way to make an entrance.

Two skinny blond kids appear out of nowhere and jump into David's arms, followed by their parents. Connie is slim, long limbed, longhaired, long nosed. Jim's features are more compact; sporting a beard, he is shorter than David but wiry. David hugs Jim, then Connie. It occurs to me I have never seen him shake hands with anyone. David is a hugger.

Jim opens the garage door and David rides the bike in. When the ignition is switched off, she heaves an audible sigh. Over these last days, I too have almost come to think of the Dove as a living thing. Now, for two days, she will rest by the long worktable, between the boys' bicycles and the two Mercedes—two merciful nights for all without threat of rain.

We remove our boots and enter the kitchen by the garage door. I am sneezing. When I stop, I hear Connie tell David how great it is that I am making this trip with him. Implied, of course, is "at her age."

The white refrigerator is covered with Post-Its. The kitchen is large, its running cabinets are all of oak. David and Jim bring in the food, wine, gifts, our luggage. I follow them to the basement stairwell, catching a glimpse of the beanbag chairs, the replicas of "original" street scenes in the living room.

Downstairs, I stumble over a skate. There is a long sofa bed. "That's where you'll sleep," David informs me. He will sleep on the foam-rubber pad on the floor. I would rather he had the more comfortable bed. He's the pilot and he most needs the rest, but I know there's no point in arguing with him.

On the stairs, the boys are fighting over the video game David brought them. Jim Jr. calls his brother "a little creep." Tom responds with "You're a big turd."

There is some professional-looking music equipment. Jim, I learn, plays in a band.

"I'll make us some fresh coffee. You're a good excuse for having it freshly brewed," Jim offers, smiling, raking his hand through his thinning hair. No sense in telling him coffee will keep me awake; I won't get much sleep anyway.

David by now has settled the argument between the boys. Tom is skating on the scratched parquet floor. Jim Jr. will teach his younger brother how to play the game when he has mastered it.

While I am glad to be here, I am feeling a little jealous of having to share a single moment of my time with David with others.

A little later, David returns from a quick shower, drying his curly hair with a towel, wearing his plaid pajama bottoms, a Christmas or birthday present from me.

"Jim says we're invited to a party tomorrow night," he says nonchalantly.

"Not me, you go. I'm sure nobody else's mother will be tagging along."

"Why do you always have to be so concerned about your age?" he says, betraying no particular irritation.

"Because I'm conditioned that way." There's a catch in my breath. "Because your Youth Generation has conditioned me."

"Ma"—his voice can be so gentle—"stop thinking of yourself as old. You're not old. I know people my age who are older than you. Anyway, I'm not going either. I don't like leaving you behind, but that's not the reason." He hesitates before he says, "Philip is coming over to see us tomorrow night."

With a thud, my heart drops right into my size-seven shoes. "I don't want to see him."

"Why not, Ma? Why can't you be friends? The difference in your ages can't be helped. Be a good sport. Wear that pretty red dress, fix your hair. We'll have some wine. Be nice. He's my friend too."

After my shower, I stand naked before the mirror. Gone the

firm breasts of my prime. Just ten years ago they wouldn't hold up a straw. Now I could tuck two pencils beneath them. My once hard, flat belly has dropped like a hem.

I put on my nightgown, come out of the bathroom, go to the open window, stand staring at the velvety dark. "Breathe in all that good air, but don't exhale. We don't need any of that Los Angeles smog," David teases. His eyes are creased with those habitually amused wrinkles.

"I bet they get some beautiful snowfalls here," I say, picturing the glistening of blues, greens, pinks on their palette of snow on a winter night.

"Come live in Canada, Ma. I can promise you snow."

I look at him. *After what happened two years ago, does he really want me to come? Or does he just want to keep an eye on his aging mother?*

But to experience winter again, and the changing seasons, is to be reminded of the light and dark of life, the inescapable cycle. I wonder if living in Southern California is making me lose my sense of that.

I go seat myself on the edge of the sofa bed. I have regretted not being more curious about my heritage while my parents were alive, so why haven't I told David some of our own family history? I feel a compulsion to tell him now.

"David, do you know why I fell in love with your father?"

He turns to me with interest.

"He reminded me of my grandfather, your great-grandfather: the same lyrical voice, the well-shaped head, the well-defined sense of self. Like your father, my grandfather read all the time. He was a scholar, a student of the Torah and the Talmud, a rabbi. He read every book he could find time for. He loved Tolstoy. He called Dickens an anti-Semite but read his books all the same. He was orthodox, never rode on Saturday or carried money on that day. Except once, when he took your grandma to the hospital. An hour later I was born."

My son is listening raptly now.

I go on. "I have one early memory. I'm in my grandfather's arms, in a huge room of dark-red walls and bright red benches. My grandfather is showing me to some bearded men. My mother takes me from him. I don't want to go. My grandfather stands on a podium and sings like a dozen songbirds. I remember a brilliant, green light over his head. His singing is accompanied by a wailing, soft and wet, like a river flowing."

"Ma, I would have loved to live out my life as a Talmudic scholar."

David's words, his face, suddenly pure and sweet, affect me like an electrical charge. Yes, it's true. David would have made a wonderful rabbi. He should have been ordained.

Friday, July 13, Colorado Springs, CO

At dawn, I wake to a house coming alive. The clock ticks, the refrigerator throbs, voices speak in undertones, someone moves quietly upstairs. Out of bed and right into the bathroom, I wash my face and hands, dress, brush my hair, put on lipstick. It feels strange not to be putting on my helmet.

Upstairs, David stands at the range flipping pancakes.

The table is set with the homemade jams and maple syrup he has brought. Connie and the boys are still in bed. Jim is working in the garage. I am aware that something is troubling me. Then I remember. Tonight I will see Philip.

Those three weeks in fantasyland had begun exactly this way, except that it was Philip who stood flipping pancakes at the range in the kitchen of our enchanted castle on the shore of the looming Pacific—a three-week windfall of precious time and space at the raw edge of the world. Even the coffee had this same dark-roasted aroma.

I met Philip when he came along with Jim to visit David, who was staying with me in Los Angeles. I had opened the windows. It was a lovely evening, jasmine perfuming the air. The men played guitar and sang, drank wine, ate my home-made potato salad. There was a quiet strength about Philip that reminded me of Leo. We had so much to say to each other.

As he was leaving, he turned to me and said quietly, "You're the woman of my dreams." It was nice for a lonely woman to hear that. "We'll meet again," he promised.

I put it out of my mind. I was, after all, not such a young woman and he was a young man.

That was ten years ago, when I looked, and felt, twenty years younger.

Two weeks later he called. There would be a ticket to San Francisco for me at the airport. Would I come?

"Yes, yes," my crooked heart cried, before the left hemisphere of my brain could intervene.

David's words bring me back to the present. "Sit and eat, Ma. You must be starved."

The boys are fighting over the other chair next to David, so I change my seat. The pancakes are delicious.

When I have a second cup of coffee, David watches without reproach. Surprisingly, last evening's coffee did not keep me awake.

After breakfast, I make a halfhearted offer to do the dishes—I'm a hurricane in my own kitchen, a disaster in others'—when all I really want to do is go down to the basement, lie across the bed, and continue basking in my daydream. "Oh good! Then I'll do something else," Connie says gratefully.

Hands in the soapy suds, I resume my daydreaming. What fun we had: the good conversation, the warmth...

Philip was tender and loving, but I learned better than to go shopping with him. All the young saleswomen were much too friendly toward him. (Or so I imagined?) We took very long walks. Each evening he built a fire. We would stare out over the ocean while we ate our lobster and wild rice and sipped our wine.

The spell was broken one evening when we went out for dinner. The waitress addressed me as "Mother."

Philip visibly blanched.

That night he said he was having "love feelings" and "love feelings" were not for us. I insisted on going to the airport the next day. I'm no beggar.

At the airport he gave me a rose wrapped in white tissue,

kissed the top of my head, and walked away. That was the last time I saw him.

Because I have promised, I give Jim Jr. a painting lesson. Working with the paints makes me hungry to paint again. We do a landscape. I instruct Jim Jr. to paint the design in the space between the plants, to look for designs in the sky, to try to use all the colors.

When we finish, I feel a need to clear my head. I ask the boy to take a walk with me.

The day is bright and clear, the wind just a breeze like a kiss on the cheek. There are mountains in every direction. With my luck it will rain tomorrow. I find myself wishing that I were on the Dove right now. I even miss being under the uncomfortable helmet. Even as it chafes, it makes me feel daring, hopeful.

As we walk by some Mexican laborers, Jim tells me, "They don't live here, they only work here."

Always the crusader, I give him a sermon, On Prejudice.

When we return to the house, the pervasive smell of roast beef is overpowering. I am slightly repelled; I seem to have absorbed some of David's abhorrence of meat. How David feels about the roast I soon find out. We eat our own food: yogurt, potatoes, a big fruit salad.

"David, I wish he weren't coming."

"Come on, Ma, be a good sport. Put on a dress."

Why should I? I don't want him to see me. He's in his prime; I'm an aging woman. My veins are sprouting like a vegetable garden; my partials don't fit so my teeth click; the circulation in my feet is so poor I have to wear socks to bed. What was I thinking ten years ago? I was needy and ashamed, shut off from the world. So I made a bold decision: not to go to my grave never tasting a man's lips again. Then I met Philip, twenty years my junior.

Age has only one recourse, to accept its condition with dignity: *To yield with a grace to reason / And bow and accept the end of a love or a season...*

At the eight-note chime of the door, I glance at the mirror, a mistake. Now that my face is broader and heavier, there are more lines in it than in the palms of my hands. I feel rotten but am thankful David is—where? The door chimes again.

"David, answer the door!" I yell.

"You answer it. I'm in the bathroom."

I straighten my shoulders and go up the stairs. Connie and Jim are off at their party. The television is on in Tom's room and Tom is fast asleep. I tiptoe in and turn it off. My heart is racing a marathon. Be still, I tell it, mind your own business, don't get involved.

At the door I take a deep breath, then another, now swing it open. *There, you've done it.* And there stands Philip, smiling, more handsome, more mellow than I remembered.

I extend my hand. "Good to see you," I lie.

"Good to see you," he says.

My lifelong need to talk now deserts me. Meditate instead, I tell myself. No, no time for that, I wish there were something, anything, I could take: a drink, a drug, a powder.

I lead him into the living room where I turn on the only softly lit lamp in the room. David is taking an awfully long time to come to my rescue. I begin thinking in desperate, defensive countermeasures: *No flash of lightning yet, the poet is lost in him. His god's eye must be missing. Anyone could see how cute I still am, cuter than ever, just as young as ever, even younger inside.*

An old Irish woman once told me to tell the truth and shame the devil. I blurt out, "Philip, there's something I want to tell you."

"What?" He's smiling again. "Your age?"

I was going to say that his teeth are much too small for his mouth. I once found that trait endearing.

He apologizes for the poor joke. "Honestly, Dorothy, I've so much wanted to tell you how the sense of fulfillment I enjoyed during our short relationship has haunted me over the years. I hope you can believe that. You know, I'm getting married soon, and in some ways, she reminds me of you."

I'll bet. That says it all. "That's wonderful. Congratulations," I say brightly.

Where the hell is my son?

"Would you like a drink?" I ask, praying he will say yes.

"Just water, if it's not too much trouble," he says, looking at me affectionately, which only increases my discomfort.

I rinse a clean glass under the kitchen faucet. How long can I reasonably take fetching him a glass of water? Long enough for David to take over? I can hear Philip twirling his keys, which with any luck means he wants to leave. I remove a bottle from the top shelf of the refrigerator and fill the glass, then add ice, quite unnecessarily, just to buy time.

Finally, I hear David enter the living room. Now I can take my time. When I return, I pause at the door. David is showing Philip the map, the route we're taking, where we have been, and where we are going. He tells him about the floods of rain, the desert heat, the dust storm. He is kind enough not to tell Philip about my getting sick.

"My BMW stood up to it all," he says, full of pride. "And so did my mother. She's a good sport. And tough. She doesn't give up."

"Your mother's quite the adventurer," Philip says, ambiguously.

David is a springboard of enthusiasm. "We're headed for some beautiful country. Hope we get some better weather. Even seasoned bikers don't like riding in bad weather."

Now I can make my entrance. I hand Philip his water. "We do have wine," I say, "and you don't need to say grace."

Philip responds with a weak smile. *Adventurer am I? What exactly did he mean by that?* I look at his hands with their light golden hairs, as he drinks his water. There was a time when those same hands were terribly exciting to me.

But give him credit for some taste, he did say knowing me was "a rich experience." And I should be thankful for the couple of moments it felt as if I were with Leo again. For that alone I should forgive him, in spite of all the fun he'll go on having while I grow frailer and die.

Have I—has anyone ever really succeeded in making the transition from lover to friend? *At any rate, you may be thankful that this is closure, the last time you will ever see each other.*

The ego can play tricks on a person. I believe I am finally beginning to accept that the world does not revolve around me. I can look forward to more such lessons at the rally.

David has his arm around my waist as we say good night. When Philip is gone, I stand at the window and look at the rectangles of yellow light in the street lamps. When I notice that David is watching me, left eyebrow eloquently cocked, I say, "Why are you looking at me like that?"

"I'm thinking that he hasn't found anyone like you and he knows it. I'm even a little sorry for him."

He follows me downstairs, helps me make up the sofa bed. Now he says, "I'm also thinking you're afraid of finding anyone who's real. And who's right for you."

"Sure, it's all right to think that way at your age," I have to remind him. "At mine, you don't take life for granted anymore. I would have liked to live out my own life with my true mate. In my case, the choice wasn't mine. I'm going to bed."

David kisses me good night.

Lying in bed, I wonder if I could have gone to my grave knowing, in the biblical sense, only one man and been happy with it. If only he had lived out a normal life span. Was Philip just the result of my losing Leo too young? Just wild, unsown oats?

A silly couplet comes to mind: *The elephant said with tears in his eyes / Why don't you pick on a fella your size?* There *was* something nice about Philip, after all.

In two weeks, we will be at David's place in Vernon. So what if I stub my toe in between every now and again? It will be good to be back there. I really ought to spend a winter there, buy some new warm clothes, ski, sleigh ride, paint the Prussian blue, green, gray night snow again.

The clock begins to strike: one ... in nature, I have read—two ... death is only an interlude in life—three ... how does one bridge the gap between the two?

SATURDAY, JULY 14, CARBONDALE, CO

David is calling me up to breakfast. I have slept late, which means another late start. The others have already eaten. I have oatmeal and coffee. "Just one cup for the road," Jim says and winks.

Everything is already packed. Today the Dove will take us to Carbondale, where David's cousin Evelyn lives.

Outside, Jim Jr. tells me, "I think I'm a good artist now. I'll send you a picture." I kiss him good-bye. More hugs and kisses all around, some picture snapping, we all say our good-byes. I put on my helmet, adjust the strap, pull it snug the way David has taught me.

The sun is out this morning. It will be good to be back in the saddle.

Little traffic this morning, the road is clear. But for some reason I'm feeling blue again. When I get like this, I recite poetry: *Into the universe, and why not knowing / Nor whence, like water, willy-nilly flowing...*

David's voice comes over the intercom: *And out of it as wind along the waste / I know not whither, willy-nilly blowing.*

David often surprises me in delightful ways.

The sky this morning is rosebud pink. Again we are zigzagging up and down the highway that crosses the Continental Divide. Reciting poetry always liberates me. "Would you like to hear more?" I ask David.

"Have I got a choice?"

"Ah love, let us be true to one another / For the world that seems to lie before us / Hath really neither joy, nor love, nor light. Matthew Arnold, 'Dover Beach.' I don't quite remember it all."

Between the day and the poetry, my spirits are improving. "What a gorgeous day! So what do you think Evelyn will think when she sees me? I know how she likes to be alone with her 'handsome, playful cousin.' Her mother tells me she adores you."

"I'm sure you'll be welcome. I don't think she wants to be alone with me, Ma. And if she does, that's her problem."

High up on Independence Pass, it's very cold; below are sheer-walled canyons, a canopy of stately firs, changing terrain that gives way to fields surging with sweet scents.

The idyll ends with our descent into uppity, touristy, snobbish Aspen. I am surprised they haven't put up gold-plated walls to keep out riffraff like us. Moneyed folks here preen themselves like human peacocks. More Pekinese canine than human actually, vain creatures decked in buttons and bows, coiffed and curled, they strut down the avenues like showgirls. We walk into an ice cream parlor, buy two tiny cones, three bucks apiece. This must be the way they keep out the hoi polloi. We sit down at a table and eat slowly, relishing the precious gelato.

"Your father could buy me an ice cream sundae for fifteen cents when we were courting."

"How did you meet him, Ma?"

"It was my high school class night. I wore my first long dress. Your grandma made it herself from a pattern. It was deep red, with roses around the neckline."

David loves hearing these stories. Before this trip, I never seemed to have the opportunity to pass them on. He moves closer.

"I was up on the auditorium platform, reciting the class poem. There was this voice behind the curtain whispering, rapid-fire, the words I had written. When I stepped back behind the curtain, I was met with this incredible smile.

"'Didn't you ever read a poem?' I asked. 'There are pauses in a poem, you know.'

"His eyes were green and slanted"—I refrain from adding *like yours.* "Then, talk about adding insult to injury, he held out his palm and offered me what looked like wriggly black ants. 'Want some breath perfumers?' That's how I met your father."

In this white-walled, sun-drenched place, I can see clearly the love in his eyes. "You must have been quite a girl," David says.

"A lot of us kids headed for Katz's Deli on the east side that night. Mama and Papa joined me, my treat, from the money I made working Saturdays at Woolworth's. The place was jammed with kids. I remember the tobacco reek competing with the smell of the corsages. Waiters were singing, 'One pastrami, two knishes, two Dr. Peppers, a ginger ale.' Boys were coughing and sputtering over their first cigarettes, and Papa was asking me, 'What are you thinking about? You're so far away.'

"'Papa,' I told him, 'something happened to change my life tonight and I don't know what it is.'"

At this moment, a real Pekinese has just pranced in, on its leash an anorexic woman in a miniskirt and four-inch heels.

Having had my fill of the local color, if not of the ice cream, I say, "Come on, David, let's get out of here before we're arrested for vagrancy."

"Whatsa matter, Ma? Don't you like slumming?"

The Dove all but bolts, leaving stagy Aspen behind. We ride first through grazing country, then through farmland, and finally into Carbondale. We meet Evelyn outside her family-sized home. She is handsome, fortyish, a bit thick in the hips. Her smile is so wide it reveals her wisdom teeth. She welcomes me. After all, I *am* her adorable cousin's mother.

The house is more impressive inside than out. There is a new stereo, a good oak table set, every convenience. Only the couch looks old and uncomfortable. She leads me to the room I will occupy: hers, the master, complete with water bed and bath with nappy bath towels.

In nearby Glenwood Springs, where Evelyn says she knows a good seafood restaurant, David parks her car on a busy street. She seems awfully worried about it. "Your car will be fine," David assures her. She smiles, suggesting great confidence in his judgment.

Over her shrimp Newburg, she asks, "What did you think of Aspen? Isn't it posh, isn't it gorgeous? Lots of famous people have homes there."

I bite my lip and refrain from saying I've heard that it's also the cocaine capital of the world. Let her keep the faith.

"I've got tickets for a dance tomorrow night, for all of us," she informs us now.

My shoulders go back, my head comes up.

"You just made my mother's day," David observes.

"She's made my tomorrow," I correct him.

My mind begins to race. It's been such a long time since I waltzed, tangoed, rumbaed. Years ago I could dance all night. Can I still glide easily in a man's arms? I will rest tomorrow, three hours at least, so I can dance all night. *Dear God, give me the opportunity just once this trip to reject an improper proposal. I promise to do it with dignity and charm.*

David leaves a hefty tip. Evelyn leaves most of her food untouched. *Silence, Dorothy!* After all, she's being very nice to me. Hasn't she just given me her bedroom?

When we leave the restaurant, it's already dark. It seems the stars have all been unpacked for the occasion of my visit. I won't believe they were already dead light-years ago.

We have come to a bench in a small, parklike area.

"Would you like to walk around the town?" Evelyn invites.

"No, thank you, Evelyn," I say, seating myself on the bench, rubbing my knee. I hate to admit it—Evelyn really is being so awfully nice, and I really would love to walk around the town—but I must get more sleep. I never seem to get enough on this trip. Once I could sleep on a crowded subway train. Now the slightest thing wakes me: the refrigerator, the plumbing, a leaky faucet.

Back home, standing before the house, the only source of light is those tender stars. "I hear water," I say to David.

"Probably a stream that feeds the Colorado. We'll explore it tomorrow."

David and Evelyn stay up, talking and laughing. I wonder as I lie in bed, listening: am I envious of Evelyn? Why should I be? Look at what I already had at her age: an adoring husband, two beautiful boys, a home of my own as nice as the one she rents.

Jealous? Me? Inadmissible.

SUNDAY, JULY 15, CARBONDALE, CO

On that bed of water that night, I dream that I am floating, light and graceful, down flights and flights of stairs. At the bottom, Leo is waiting, his eyes full of admiration.

When I open my eyes, it's dawn. I wish I could go back to the dream, but David has just announced breakfast. I take a sixty-second shower and dress quickly.

Entering the breakfast nook, I sing out at the plentiful sunshine pouring in through the wide window, "*Lux fiat*. Let there be light."

The weather is always gorgeous when we are not on the road.

There are pancakes already on the table. David makes more, while Evelyn jazzes up some beaten eggs with diced tomato, peppers, and cheese. She is beaming at David as he works at the range. I thank her for her hospitality. "I'm sure this is the best sleep I'll get until we get to Vernon."

She flashes me a lovely smile and says, "I'm glad you enjoyed your sleep," then rivets her whole attention back on David. *It's almost uncanny,* I think, then dismiss the troubling association.

Breakfasting like this is sheer luxury. When I have eaten the last pancake, I ask, "Are we going to take that walk, David?"

"Do you mind if I take Evelyn for a ride on the motor-cycle? She'd really like to go, Ma."

Taken somewhat aback, I say, "No, I don't mind." (Not much, anyway.) I decide to put a good face on it. "I'll just rest up, do my nails. Do you have some eye makeup I can borrow?"

"Sure. There's some in the bathroom drawer under the sink. Help yourself."

Though she does not wear lipstick, her eyes always look made-up. Good thing she admitted to having eye makeup; otherwise, it would have been hard for me not to say something.

I watch David helping her into my leather jacket and my helmet, which fits her better than me. "Have a good time," I say, "and be careful." For good measure, I throw in another, "Be careful, all right?"

Using the tone she probably reserves for hysterical

mothers, Evelyn says wearily, "He'll be all right. He's in good hands."

"Oh I'm sure he's in good hands—now that you have him all to yourself."

Oh my. Did I really say that?

Evelyn looks perplexed. "You're kidding, right? You can't mean that."

I don't dare now look at David.

David says, "Even when she says something mean, she means it."

Now, how unfair, how grossly unfair! Did I make a fuss about missing our walk? *So I worry about my son. Is that so awful?*

My hands are trembling. I bolt for the bedroom and lie down on the quivering water bed. *Couldn't David have said something to lighten things up? Mark would have, even if I had been mean.*

I haven't taken my estrogen—can that be it?

When I'm upset like this, I sleep.

When I wake hours later, they're still not back. *Worry, worry, worry—life is a gulf of grief.* Instead of grieving, I decide to take that walk, find that stream.

I amble along past small summer cottages for summer people, their big cars in the carports, their horses, cows, goats, sheep in the meadows. I've had little actual contact with animals in the course of my lifetime—mostly through Papa's stories about them and about sunsets, his vague tales of milkmaids and farmers' daughters, from the days when he hopped freights and found jobs on farms. Being young meant that someday you'd escape the slums, live in the country, in a country house, with the white piano Papa had promised me. Then, as now, youth is promised all the prizes.

There's the stream. How far? Still, I never felt deprived as a child, Papa's imagination could transform our slum world into a menagerie, a forest green with hope.

I turn back toward the house, giving myself time before my worry program begins to run.

Back at Evelyn's, they still haven't returned. *I know, I'll get dressed, that will take up some time before I pitch into the Abyss of Worry.* I do my nails, find the eye makeup, apply it carefully, fix my hair, find a flattering mirror that doesn't face the window and the light.

Not bad, not too bad, I must remember to keep my shoulders straight. I am out of calcium pills, my estrogen is low, but the revolving low lights should help. *No one will ask me to dance anyway—I might as well be invisible like Harvey, the pooka.*

I really shouldn't have spoken to Evelyn that way. I think of David's face, the way it clouded over.

At long last, they return, laughing. They've been having a good time. Met some of Evelyn's friends—that's what took so long. Was I worried? What? Me—worry?

Overruled.

David has put on the red plaid Pendleton shirt I love on him. Evelyn comes out in faded jeans, a coarse-woven shirt in a green I could never wear. I feel dated in the red dress that has hung for so long in my closet. "Red is your color, Gypsy," Leo used to say, buying me red robes, red night-gowns, even a red wool suit. These days, I really do prefer peaceful, warm yellow-greens to wild, racy reds. I take one last look in the mirror before I follow David and Evelyn out.

In town we eat at a Mexican restaurant up the block from the dance hall. The food is none too good, the rice gummy and cold. People on their way to the dance stop to greet David and Evelyn.

When we leave and start up the street, I note the bridge lined with yellow goblets of lights.

My pulse has begun to race with anticipation. The dance, at least, is something to look forward to. Tonight I am going to trot, even tango maybe, make this red dress glow, have a grand time. A romantic evening out.

That's what I think.

As it turns out, the dance hall reeks of smoke, sweat, cheap perfume, licentiousness. The band is loud, brassy, discordant. Everyone looks under forty. They have probably never heard of the tango, waltz, foxtrot. A good clap of thunder would sound better than what here passes for music.

Still, because the beat does get into my feet, I step onto the dance floor with David. Trouble is, the music also reaches my ears. Fifteen minutes pass and I've had it. "Dance with Evelyn," I order him. "I'm going to take a walk, explore the other wonders of this town."

"Don't go too far away. We probably won't stay very long."

When Evelyn sees me leaving, she heads me off. "If you

walk over the bridge, you can see the Glenwood Hot Springs Mineral Baths. It's the largest in the world." She gives me a generous smile that I do not deserve. I can be grateful.

Walking on the bridge, the cool, refreshing night air calms my nerves. I stop to look over the railing at the mysterious green waters under their soft lights. Young couples leap, dive, splash, gambol, frolic, laugh, spark in the honeymoon haven below. The wind has drowned out the cacophony of the band—"zydeco" they call it—not for me, I know now.

I stand and watch them much too long, until I can stand it no longer and the yearning overwhelms me.

The very last time Leo and I made love, there was as much pain and anger between us as there was love. We were saying good-bye with our bodies, violently but also tenderly. We were losing each other, and we knew it. At the instant of climax, a sob escaped me.

During the last few days of his life, there were only the twining of fingers, of toes, left to remind us.

With the sleeve of my dress I brush away my tears. This impractical memory of yours—now where have you left your glasses, your wallet this time? he was always asking. My absentmindedness has been a constant torment. Poor Leo. I was such a forgetful, extravagant, inept wife. *You were cheated out of half a lifetime, my darling.*

They're out looking for me now. I guess they've had enough, or David has anyway. Like us, his father and me, he loves the classics, the old jazz.

We do have to leave early in the morning. I'm sorry for David. We have a long haul ahead, and the couch he has been sleeping on is too short, hard, and uncomfortable. After I get into bed, I listen for a while to David and Evelyn's low, murmuring voices before I drift off.

MONDAY, JULY 16, ESTES PARK, CO

I wake earlier than usual, only to discover that David seems to be gone. I search the house, even the basement. Finally— it's getting rather late—I knock lightly on Evelyn's door, then open it. "Sorry to wake you, but I can't seem to find—"

Very discreetly, I close the door and return to my room. Subject closed.

Later as we wave good-bye to Evelyn, I note how much she is already beginning to resemble her mother. She has told David she hopes to visit him in British Columbia. Not on my watch, I hope.

Passing through Hot Sulphur Springs, skirting another national forest, we begin our climb once more.

Coming across a branch lying in our path, instead of going around, David pulls off the road, removes the branch from the road, and carefully deposits it on the forest floor, on a mound of mossy fallen branches and rotting leaves.

Negotiating the hairpin turns of a Continental Divide highway, we're on the last leg of our journey to the rally. With a sharp intake of breath, I can really feel the cold now. It makes me sit up and remember: Winter evenings in New

York, I would lie next to David, sing him to sleep, then hurry to dress for a party so I could watch Leo shave. Such delight it gave me, I don't know why. I would sit on the bath- tub ledge and watch as he lathered his face with the shaving soap. I loved the way he firmed his chin to get into its deep cleft. We had our finest talks then.

Cold itself does not bother me; in fact, it helps to make me more alert. It is the heat that slows my mental processes. I realize how I have missed the briskness of a real winter, its preservative quality.

It's said you have to go to strange places to find yourself anew. Arms encircling my grown child, I thread through the landscape on the back of a dove, and the doors of memory are flung wide.

We are traveling through Rocky Mountain National Park, elevation 11,500 feet. In the everlasting struggle of life for survival, hardy spruce and pine here at this altitude grow sideways and become dwarfish.

In my childhood, the most beautiful place in the world, to me, was Eastern Parkway, with its cordon of trees running up the median, separating the apartment dwellings from the affluent brownstones on the other side. I had friends living there, with their oriental rugs and grand fireplaces, their music of violins, pianos, older sisters singing "Sweet mys- tery of life…" like exquisite captives yearning only to escape. Sunday mornings, I would stand under those trees, listen- ing to the violins, wishing I owned one. I never did.

Last year, I watched a man weave down the stairs of

one of those burnt-out, boarded-up brownstone wrecks, watched him urinate in the alleyway between the houses, and suddenly I felt I knew what death was. It was there in that alley.

On our descent, I massage David's back. He slumps forward, just relaxing, as he has reassured me before. But how can I be sure? I worry that I am putting him to sleep.

All around us now is blue fir, blue columbine. I see swallows, sparrows, birds I don't recognize. I should have brought a bird book along; my ignorance appalls me.

Soon it will be August. And here it will already be winter.

We are riding into a fairyland, an enchanted forest. Elves certainly must inhabit this greenery. A giant must have hewn out the rock and placed this quaint village inside the jagged mountain that frames it.

I talk into the open intercom. "David, this is a stone's throw from heaven."

"I know. That's why we're here. I wanted you to see it."

This is Estes Park.

It reminds me of another faraway town long ago when a small boy and his mother spent a summer together and became friends. It is my earnest prayer that one day on this trip we will rediscover that summer together. But it must be his own memories David recalls.

The Dove rolls smoothly to a stop in one of the unmetered parking spots. I jump off.

"Getting good at that," David compliments me.

I remove my helmet. People mill about, cheerful, relaxed,

as if on holiday. They smile at us, ask where we have been, where we are going. The breeze is like velvet on my cheeks. "If I lived here," I tell David, "I'd feel as if I were on vacation all the time."

"You can move up to Canada anytime you want. It's just as lovely," he reminds me.

The street is lined with small, freestanding storefronts under different colored awnings. Under a green one, there's a much too cute window display: set in a miniature alpine landscape of snow drifts against a backdrop of mountains, stuffed animals nibble at wheels, hunks of cheeses and breads.

The store is run by two attractive, dark-haired girls. Cheese samples are likewise cutely marked, "Try me." The girls ogle David, who smiles back. The bolder of the two says, "You can sample anything in the store." She is big bosomed, tiny waisted, narrow hipped.

No novice in such matters, David says slyly, "Anything?"

"Anything. Even what isn't labeled."

The nerve. Yet, I confess to a twinge of envy.

My fountain of youth may have run dry, but my appetite remains vigorously healthy. David is my unwitting accomplice. And with the other girl now into the act and both so engrossed in vying for his attention, I could make off with a half wheel of blue cheese. I try every sample in the shop.

David is buying four kinds of cheese and some sourdough bread, and is taking his sweet time about it. I might as well be chewing on a lemon. But I hold my tongue.

I can be grateful that at least he hasn't taken telephone

numbers, meaning more expensive, long-distance calls. He gives the girls that sexy wink and that wave of his, and that smile that comes so naturally to him. The transparency, the stark simplicity of the come-on—still, to be fair, I remind myself we are all born of lust.

On our way out, a gray-haired couple holding hands stop us to ask if we need a place for the night. David shakes out his map. "No, but you wouldn't know of any campgrounds we can get to by dark, would you?"

"Sure, there it is, Chugwater," says Dad, smiling, pointing at the map. "Didn't we enjoy that place, Sal?"

Sal smiles back. "Well, Dad, they may find it a bit uncomfortable."

I like these people. If we had a bumper sticker, Honk If You Like Jews, they would honk.

"We'll try it," David says.

They wave as we ride off. Both thin and tall, they look very much alike, very much made for each other. It makes me feel sad. How beautiful growing old together might have been.

We ride on for a long time until the clouds slowly begin to gather for another storm.

"Not more rain, David?" I groan into the intercom.

"We ride in, we ride out" is his blithe answer.

There are just a few drops, and then a long peaceful stretch. We pass a town with the unlikely name of Loveland; I start singing "Dreamland, Dreamland," one of Papa's favorites. He used to sing it as he puttered around in our tiny apartment, fixing a leaky faucet or setting a mousetrap.

Mama would lend her tinny voice to his. *"Meet me tonight in dreamland..."*

I remember a photo of her, in profile, her eyes large and dark, her dark hair in a heavy bun lying against the nape of her neck. She wears a lacy, cream-colored gown, cut low, but not improperly so, and a red rose on her bosom.

A vague memory, of dancing a Viennese waltz with Papa, comes back to me. He is wearing the silk shirt and spats that lay in his old brown trunk for years. Strange. He never wore them after he married.

What if they were both to come back to life, to this world with its movies that reveal everything, the tell-all books, the no-holds-barred talk shows, the billboards that impertinently dictate the use of a condom? Papa, with his romantic sensibility, would deplore it. Mama, full of common sense, would just laugh, aware that the world has indeed at last gone utterly mad.

It was not a sweeter world then. Nevertheless, I have always had this hankering to have been born a hundred years earlier. That's me, a thoroughly modern 1890s woman. Give me gaslight and horse-drawn carriages.

We are bypassing Greeley, where Mark taught at the university for a year. He had a lovely four-room apartment there on university grounds. I visited him once for three weeks; it was like living in a park, in the midst of a flirtation of birds. Except for an old table and chairs, a desk, and a bed, the apartment was bare. I bought a dozen pillows and made some lamps out of bottles. We invited the whole psychology department over for wine and cheese and danced to Mark's records.

A visiting professor from Jordan asked me to marry him. "Naturally," I replied, "you want to stay in the States, get a green card. And then what? Will you poison me?"

The memory makes me laugh, even with the walloping we're now taking from another thunderstorm. David once said, "Our vulnerability to the elements is part of the beauty of the experience."

The storm too makes me laugh at myself: that crazy old lady on the motorcycle!

A wrong turn, a bum steer, or a blink, and we have missed Chugwater!

Banishing rain and wind, the sun has overleapt the sky and now crouches between the trees, as it settles in for the night. I forget for the moment that I am a malcontent at heart, always yearning for change. Darkness falls, and I am glad just now to be alive on this good, green earth, beneath this ancient sky so proud with stars.

This contentment soon yields to my habitual apprehensiveness. David has anticipated this; over the intercom he tells me, "We'll stop in Wheatland instead," then adds, "Wyoming is so flat here, it's boring."

Not sorry to hear this, I say, "It'll be too late to find camping grounds. Let's get a room, or we'll be riding another fifty miles in the dark. Besides, you know I was born incontinent."

The first innkeeper is square faced, all blubber, liver lips, and a potbelly, which he keeps scratching. He spits out his consonants, leers at me, looks me straight in the chest, and grinds out, "Even for an hour of pleasure I got no rooms."

I use my thumb to signal David, Away, away! I tell him as we leave, "He was picking his nose when we came in."

"I know, I saw. Maybe he had something in his eye?"

We both laugh. Leo once said the same thing.

At the next motel, I wait for David on the Dove, as instructed, till he comes out smiling. "The town owns some campgrounds. No charge."

Less than fifteen minutes later, we are in the park. David sets up the tent, inflates the mattress, and opens the flaps up to the night. This is what camping should always be. We can see the arch of the sky as easily as if we were sleeping right under it. The moon is full tonight. The leaves lisp. The earth smells fruity, faintly reminiscent of licorice.

Papa would have said, "God must be rolling the dice tonight." An afterlife of gambling—that was his idea of heaven. On the Saturday afternoon he was told he had a new daughter, a neighbor had found him in the basement with his fellow sinners. Later, he would shake his head, gray eyes catching the light, and ruefully say, "That was the only time I was ever lucky."

Papa always said he had won me in a crap game.

Tonight I'm wearing the green flannel nightgown I bought for this trip, which, so far, I have worn only on our nights in. I cannot help thinking about the two girls in Estes Park.

"David, you know I really wish you would open up more,"
I say for openers, apropos of nothing. "You're so private in
your feelings that I have to nag. The sun rises and sets again
before I can get you to say anything."

David, of course, remains silent. I sigh, wondering if my
words have fallen once again on deaf ears.

"David," I try again, getting to what is really on my mind,
"those two girls, how did they know you weren't my lover?"

"Jeeze, Ma!" And he seems genuinely horrified, which I
don't find precisely flattering.

I persist. "Still, you know they would have been just as
flirtatious. Really, David, there's such a prejudice against an
older woman and a young man. It really hasn't changed, in
spite of the whole feminist movement. It sure is different
when the roles are reversed. Would you have been ashamed
of me if I was an older woman, not your mother?"

David lifts his head and fixes me with a this-I-can-handle
gaze. "I'm not sure, Ma. It's crossed my mind. Once in a
while an older woman appears, and I find myself wishing she
were my age. I have a feeling an older woman could make me
happy. I don't know if I'm crazy enough. Or sane enough."

"Or man enough?"

I like the way David laughs: a rumbling baritone that
comes up from his chest and turns a silky tenor in his throat.

It's only a little later—we are eating our dinner of
Camembert, yogurt, peaches, sourdough bread—when it
happens: he begins to remember what I have so hoped he
would on this trip.

"I'll never forget that summer you and I became best friends. Remember, Ma? The summer we spent at the St. George, in Brooklyn Heights, while the house was being renovated. I was your only child that summer. You had time for me. I loved you so much then."

And now? I wonder. *Has that time passed?* Something stirs in me. It's a baited trap. I sidestep it. "No cooking, no cleaning, just time with you," I say instead, remembering how Leo had left early, worked long hours, and always came back after David's bedtime. "It's one of my loveliest memories, how you'd be dressed and in the lobby by seven, and I had to hurry after you. You know me. I couldn't let you go it alone."

We listen for a moment to the warbling of birds, the soft lapping of the lake.

David is laughing now. "I never dressed that quickly for school! I couldn't wait to get down there."

"Your first year in business and you weren't quite five. A stick of gum with a song and dance to go along. It was a pretty sharp idea, and you were so cute in your black shorts with the white shirt and red bow tie."

"You let me keep the dimes, but you made me give back the quarters and the halves."

"You were so disappointed when I said, 'No, not even the quarters.'"

"I'd made all kinds of plans for what I'd do with the money."

"But soon you looked up at me and you said, 'I don't really care, Ma. I make them laugh.' You couldn't have kept all that money anyway, David. You would have had to pay income tax."

David shrugs. "After a while I didn't mind. I loved those people."

"And what you did for those lonely people! Remember when we first came, how they sat there like dried autumn leaves, rustling their papers, pretending to read, too shy to speak? Then you became the subject of conversation, and they became so casual, so easy with each other. I bet a couple of romances developed because of you. Say, did you give our phone number to that traveling salesman?"

"Sure. He was the most generous. He was my friend, and he asked for it."

"Sure, sure, David."

"Why? Did he bother you, Ma?"

"I could handle him. Only one of those people caused me some worry."

David's voice suddenly saddens. "Hart McCullen. That's who you mean, isn't it? I loved him. He was my favorite. He took me into his room and showed me how the tattooed nudes danced on his muscles. He told me stories."

"Hairy stories, I'm sure. He gave you chunks of chocolate when you refused his dollars."

"I loved his stories, though I don't remember them."

"I'll bet. You wouldn't repeat them. You never repeated anything."

I am massaging David's back. He rolls his head and relaxes his muscles as he remembers. "Those foghorns seemed to be moaning, begging, 'Come away, come far away with me.' The church bells sent out another message. 'Stay here, stay here, or I'll miss you.'"

Brooklyn Heights was called the City of Churches. Every Sunday, we attended the one with the best choir. It was once a seafaring town, before the mansions that belonged to sea captains became boarding houses, before the carriage houses, brownstones, stables were renovated, remodeled, rendered commonplace.

David is stroking my arm. "Ma, I was so proud of you in those big hats you wore."

"Remember how we took down the snow scene in our room, and you said, 'They should hang the artist!' I thought that was so funny. And then we hung Hopper's *A View from the Bridge*." Our beloved bridge—the Brooklyn, of course—depicted with the green hills in the background. The painting all but transformed the vapid gold and white interior of our suite.

Each morning, after David went downstairs, I would sit in front of the mirror and ponder what I would wear that day. I dressed carefully. After all, I had an ongoing date with my best beau (and that is where my daily responsibilities began and ended). I would take the elevator down to the lobby, where I would stand and listen to his high, sweet voice, and my heart would stop, watching him there in the floating dust motes of the morning sun, singing his own heart out. When I heard the applause, that was my cue to come for him. The guests would be sitting, smiling, looking less careworn than before.

Always so gregarious, David didn't seem to miss the other

children that summer. It was just he and I in a world of adults.

After that, holding hands, we would walk out into the streets. "What else did you sing today?" I would ask.

"'Annabelle Lee,' and whatever else they asked for."

David had a whole repertoire of Scotch, Irish, and Jewish songs my father had taught him. As we walked toward the bridge, all along the way people would stop to talk to David: the dentist in his white coat, the old men tapping their canes and humming songs, the dainty ladies returning from breakfast at Schraft's.

At the foot of the bridge was a small grocery run by one of the old seamen who stayed at the St. George. We would buy a brown bag of green split peas and walk up on the bridge. Even on the hottest days it was cool there.

The birds learned to recognize us, brought along their families, and ambushed us. Settling on our heads, arms, shoulders, they ate out of our palms until the peas were gone.

"Smart little creatures," David would remark.

"Bandits, freeloaders," I used to say.

"I never kept any of that money," David reminds me now.

True, David would throw the dimes he earned into the river—all of them, until he ran out—and the teenage boys would dive for them from the decks of the boats below. These performances made us laugh. After a while, I started letting David keep the quarters; it seemed a shame to watch these boys diving only for dimes. And they loved the pay increase!

"Always the big spender," I say.

David's voice now becomes smaller and younger, as if he were that boy again. "The best part was when we got to the other end of the bridge in lower Manhattan and had breakfast in that small cafe. The waitress was pretty and blond. I remember she had arms that looked like they had been lathered with whipped cream."

"And after you kissed her, she would slip you a glass of buttermilk, 'on the house.'" This makes me laugh now. "You sure learned young."

"I remember her husband too, the chef, tossing dough into the air. Every time I hear Gilbert and Sullivan, I see him: white apron, white toque, singing his heart out."

After breakfast, we always walked to the Fulton Street Fish Market to watch the fishermen bringing in their catch. David always wanted to throw them back into the sea.

"Poor fish," he says. "They were so blue and cold. I couldn't stand to see them struggle in the net."

Then back across the bridge we'd go, the newsboys singing out the daily news.

There was one day, the one blemish on the entire summer. "Ma, remember that day when we walked into the lobby and I saw the hearse driving off? I was so scared, like I already knew what had happened. When the people in the lobby told us Mr. McCullen had dropped dead of a heart attack, I was sick. I just ran."

"And I chased after you. Found you in one of those sand piles at the Esplanade, dirty and tear stained."

I remember how his mouth quivered. "You'll die too," he cried, almost an accusation.

"Not for a long time," I promised him. "And by then I'll be tired and just want to go to sleep forever."

David is cutting an apple. "What's worse than finding a worm in your apple?" he asks, giving me half.

"I heard that one before you were born." Shall I say I knew a lot of things before he was born? Instead I say, "You were such a joy, David."

I am beginning to get drowsy. I yawn, even as I wish this night would never end. That imaginary cup of memories has finally brimmed and run over. I feel confident that here in this tent, in this mythical place beneath this proscenium lit with stars, the prospect of dying seems far off, farther away than it has seemed in a long time. I pray for one thing: *God, please take me after a good night's sleep. After that, I can handle anything.*

TUESDAY, JULY 17, MOUNT RUSHMORE, SD

David is trying to explain. "The birds start fighting for territory before dawn—"

"Those are mating calls," I protest, coming to their defense. I have been awakened this morning by a rush of wings and raucous bird cries.

"All right, Ma," he says, "then have it your way. Let them keep their secrets."

I get up, stretch, and head for the showers, the sky already lit up. The facility is clean, the water is hot, and there's plenty of soap. While I shower, I bask in the memory of last night's talk.

Back at the tent, David surprises me as I sit and dry my hair. "I have something to show you."

"Omigod." They're photos. "When did you have those developed?"

"When we were at Evelyn's. Come on, have a look."

"Forget it, David." Growing old gracefully is not a process that lends itself to film.

"Come on, Ma. You look sweet."

"Me, sweet?"

"You can be." He strokes my hair. He bends down and kisses me. Gratefully, I kiss him back.

I take the photo and look at it: me, asleep. None of the usual self-consciousness, I look as contented as a fetus in the womb.

"Now was that so bad?" he asks when I hand the photo back.

"Do that again, David, and next time I just may turn you to stone."

After David has repacked the Dove in his usual efficient manner, we're off to Mount Rushmore and the rally. We will be spending the next three nights in David's promised land.

Contrary to expectation, Wyoming is not at all flat! There are rolling grasslands dotted with farms and ranches, sun-shod rivers full of the juice of life. I am still happy from the night before, from the long talk and the reliving of that unforgettable summer.

"David," I say over the intercom, "you could pan for gold in this air."

When he raises a gloved hand, as if to touch mine, I have a fleeting recollection of the bright, gentle little boy full of charm and pluck, in his red bow tie. This is immediately followed by an unexpected sadness that touches me like the faintest of breezes: I love the man, but miss the boy.

Just to remind me that nothing is forever, the sun sneaks off and the sky begins to sulk. We slide into deafening wind and rain.

With a deadline to meet, David insanely refuses to slacken the pace, even to change into our rain gear. I mustn't let him know I'm frightened.

Finally coming to his senses, he pulls off the highway. We stop at a restaurant. Sunny days, we can stop and go as he pleases. Inclement weather invariably makes me hungry. He unpacks our rain gear and hands me my canary suit.

Inside the restaurant he finds us a table near the window. I go to the rest room, lay my helmet on the sink before I wash my hands and clean my wraparound sunglasses.

A skinny blonde at the sink next to mine is studying me in the mirror. "You traveling alone?"

Her question annoys me, why exactly I can't say. "No," I curtly reply and hurry away. Maybe because they're still subjects of the moon, raunchy younger women don't particularly appeal to me. Envy has nothing to do with it. Anyway, how much better off I am, I think, in this era of AIDS. No hits, no runs, but also no errors.

David has already ordered: cereal and juice for him. I order French toast and coffee.

"Half a dozen cups, Ma?" he needles me.

"You know, I rarely make coffee at home anymore."

"If I were Catholic, that's what I'd give up for Lent."

"David, you're a brat."

As usual, we attract attention. Three men in cowboy hats at the next table watch us as if we were *Harold and Maude*. Across the room a child of five is sucking on a salt shaker. David's eyes follow mine. "I think I'll give up salt for Lent instead," I tell him. I think of David coming home from school at that age, whistling Bach.

I can feel his excitement building when he says, "We'll get to Mount Rushmore while it's still light. The Rapid City fairgrounds are only about twenty miles from there."

The way he's been driving, that shouldn't take more than fifteen minutes, I imagine, but say nothing.

The rain now is coming down so hard it's bouncing off the pavement. "Look, David," I say, "I think the sky is falling."

Ignoring the remark, he eyes the headline in someone's *New York Times*. A squat little man looks up and grunts, "Time for another war."

David smiles broadly. "And with our technology, we can make a bigger and better one this time."

Noisily, the man rattles his newspaper. "Yep," he grunts again—end of conversation.

"Today's the day Noah sails away on his ark," I continue.

"We'll have to pass, Ma. No room for the Dove."

The French toast is good, thick, and nicely browned on

both sides. I am already anticipating a bout of depression: three days at the rally, David always the center of attention, and I will be the alien, the pariah, baring my fangs, wrinkling my crow's feet at all the youngsters.

"Speaking of wars, David, do you remember that aristocratic lady, the retired professor who watched the Vietnam documentary with us? Remember how shocked she was by the posters that read "Pull Out, Dick?" She said, 'Imagine calling the president by his first name.'"

"You get the innuendo, don't you, Ma?"

"Of course I do. David, am I supposed to pretend to an innocence I don't have?"

David apologizes unnecessarily. "Sorry, I didn't mean it that way, Ma."

There, I have overreacted again. Always this feeling I'm being censured, subtly and not so subtly. Always this feeling of being misunderstood. *You're acting paranoid again,* I scold myself. What more could I want than this son of mine who has changed my life from a minor to major key? A lover? Or just a hot fudge sundae?

"It's just that I don't understand you sometimes," I explain, guiltily.

"I'm just preparing you, Ma. You'll be hearing plenty of obscenities at the rally, and there won't be any dashes between the first and fourth letters."

"You don't talk that way."

"A lot of these guys do. I guess I don't because my father taught me that profanity is the effort of a limited mind to express itself."

David refills our water glasses, and then picks up the rose I have filched from a bush in front of the restaurant. "Ma, life is such a mishmash. We need something to believe in. This is what has meaning for me," he says, holding up the rose. "I believe in God and his creation. Leo didn't believe."

"Leo had God in his heart," I hasten to say.

"All right, Ma, but he never looked God in the eye."

"Would there really be more justice in our lives if we all believed?" I wonder aloud, as I study his hair: thick, curly, and three shades past blond.

"I don't know. Einstein believed. He said, 'If God metes out punishment and reward, isn't he also passing judgment on himself?'"

A little later when we are leaving the restaurant, I witness a scene between mother and the salt-shaker-sucking five-year-old, now on the verge of tears. She's warning him, "You better straighten out that face or I'll really give you something to cry about."

David smiles, mischievously. "Another salt shaker maybe?"

Outside, he's reassuring me, "Ma, we'll be in Mount Rushmore in about three hours. You're in for a treat."

I'm already having my treat. I take his arm now and squeeze. "David, you've given some meaning back to my life. I just want you to know that."

The last leg of our trip to the rally is interrupted by another of my panic attacks. While the rain is only spotty now, there is still no reason for David to speed, as he casually gesticulates at the sights. I tap him on the shoulder and he pulls over.

"What now, Ma?"

"David, being with you now doesn't calm my fears for the times when I won't be with you."

"Now what's that supposed to mean?"

"It means you sure know how to make a mother worry."

"Look, Ma! You know, I've really just about had it up to here!" His voice is brusque and bruising. "For God's sake, will you just for once lay off?"

Back on the road, he's taking it somewhat slower. The Wizard said it would take more than imagination to get Dorothy back to Kansas. Words to live by. Will I finally learn? Leo used to say, "They come through you, not from you."

Must I learn to stop thinking of David as my child?

As we climb the winding highway, David points out the monumental portraits in stone as they come into view. My breath quickens. Goosebumps rise at the sight of these eloquent, statuesque faces growing more massive as we climb higher. The representation is so keen, the faces seem almost to come alive: Lincoln's warmth and compassion, Washington's paternal concern for his fellow citizens, Jefferson boldly—and significantly?—facing west, with Roosevelt seemingly nodding his hearty approval. I feel pride in a mankind capable of sculpting in stone, for coming generations to enjoy and ponder, this gigantic record of its sometimes equally gigantic achievements.

When we have reached the top, David parks the Dove next to two other BMWs. The running engine of the bike right next to the Dove is making a sound like castanets. A tall, thin girl, the rider evidently, looks troubled. Her companion sits on his bike, sheepish and helpless.

David goes for his tools. That's my son: with a wrench he can repair the world. He kneels down next to the bike and soon has it running smoothly again. "Loose tappets," he explains. "If you hear that noise again, take care of it immediately, or it will ruin your engine."

The girl smiles. "Thank you so much."

Her sullen companion doesn't even acknowledge David's presence.

"See you at the rally," David says, under the impression that he has made two new friends.

As they walk off, the girl looks back and waves. Her thinness is accentuated by the matching belt cinching the hem of her short black leather jacket.

On the observation deck, there are hordes of people with cameras snapping pictures. One man in a wheelchair is wearing only a ribbed undershirt, the black hair on his chest showing. Young girls walk along clad only in shorts and tube tops. How can they stand it? It's like the Siberian tundra here and these people have come dressed for a pool party.

"Ma, stand there. I wanna take your picture."

"I'm freezing, David."

This trivial rite over with, I read the various plaques to keep myself warm. In the fourteen years it took to complete the project, not a single worker was killed, although they did have to contend with the cruel moods of the South Dakota winters.

"Not to mention the summers," I mutter to myself.

David now points out a mountain goat strolling over Lincoln's beard. This he must have a picture of!

"We going to wait until he visits all the monuments?"

"And watch you turn to ice?" David laughs.

Children share bags of popcorn and caramels as they walk along, or ride on the shoulders of their fathers. I saw Leo do this many times. A four-year-old tugs at his father's shirt-tail. "Carry *me* now." Father kisses the smaller child, sets her down, and picks up the older.

When I start to enter the ladies' room, a man asks me to accompany his child. The girl is tousle-haired and has a fresh, perky little face.

When we come back out, he says, "Did you say thank you?"

"Naw," the little girl drawls, "she was making peepee too."

Fresh, indeed. The sky is darkening again, threatening an avalanche of rain.

"This park deserves more time," David tells me. "We'll come back one night and see the monuments when they're lit up."

I can hardly wait.

The Rally

After a quick sprint through Rapid City and out, up into the heights on the outskirts of town, we have arrived at the fairgrounds, beating the rain and the odds of incurring a casualty. Dismounting, I suddenly realize how tired I am. I think, if only I could take this excitement intravenously. I need a chair, badly.

Despite my fatigue, suddenly it's a kick just to be here; there is already a palpable and infectious excitement in the air. We are met at the entry to the event by a long line of folding tables set up against a city-block-long backdrop of blue-and-white bunting. Two men in green visors show David where to park his bike. Other men are arriving with folding chairs, but these are strictly for the people collecting our fees.

While I wait in line to pay my $44 fee by check, David signs up for classes at another table. From where I stand, shoulders hunched, waiting my turn, I can see David scanning a list, probably for names of people he knows. All the noise now somehow reminds me of a day-care center yard. Someone in the vicinity seems to be suffering from flatulence.

Except for the bearded ones, it is hard to tell the men from the women, not least because of the identical way both sexes are dressed. From the attention they are getting, I can discern that some, although not many, are female. The women all seem awfully body-conscious. All these smooth young faces still unetched by the lines of harsher experience—they act tough, but with their white teeth, soiled T-shirts, and dirty talk, they are no more worrying than a busload of high school students.

Then I think to myself, *still you're like a vestal virgin at a Dionysian bacchanal*, and I smile.

There is distant thunder that has steadily been growing in volume. I had hoped we would be settled before the rain could strike, but no such luck. A sudden squall leaves me soaked and shivering. David has momentarily disappeared, making me feel abandoned and wretchedly alone, like a seagull circling a deserted beach, its shadow lengthening across the sand with every long, slow pass. And I'm still waiting in line.

After paying my fee, I find David. Just following him around now, afraid to lose sight of him, I keep looking to him to show some pity toward his poor, old mother. But there he goes again, talking tappets, rods, crankshafts, shock absorbers, oil pumps, exhaust pipes. I'd have a better chance of getting his attention if I were made of chrome or covered in grease.

Now he's talking to a slight, helpless little thing in cutoffs so short one can see the white half-moons of her buttocks.

The tiredness will simply not go away. Just a little space, some silence, I tell myself, a place to lay my head—that's all I need. But first, we have to locate our group. Until then, we cannot set up our tent.

At last, when I can take it no longer, I steal up behind him and tug at his sleeve. "David, I'm tired," I almost whine.

"Sorry, Ma." Then he says to the girl, "It'll have to wait until tomorrow."

How I *do* hate this distress, this feeling sorry for oneself, this dogged fatigue that comes with age, that reduces one to the condition of a helpless child.

BRITISH COLUMBIA, WELCOME! reads the large banner.

Through the iron bars of the fence running along the Canadian camp at the far back of the fairgrounds, I can see a horse path. The smell of horse dung is strong but not offensive.

David quickly sets up the tent and inflates the mattress. I stand helplessly by, without even breath enough to help, my boots stuck in the mud. When David finishes, he yanks my boots off and deposits them on newspapers inside the tent. I crawl inside, drawing my legs in behind, and collapse on the mattress.

Outside, I hear Michael greet David warmly. This is followed by the sounds of the two setting up Michael's tent. Off in the background, motorcycles buzz like chain saws. David tells a man called Ben, "I'll check your valve clearances to-morrow and make sure the carburetor adjustments are correct."

I wonder if Ben can stand the suspense.

David throws open the flaps of the tent now. "Ma, I want you to meet Ben and Teresa."

Ben, it turns out, is David's chiropractor, and so young looking that I'm not sure that Teresa isn't his mother. I sit up and say hello. She is actually very pretty and plump, with eyes the color of dark rum. They have come on two bikes, with their two children in sidecars.

No use fighting it, I've got to get up now and go to the outhouse. The toilets and shower rooms are some distance away, I discover. Welcome British Columbia, my gluteus maximus.

I pull on my muddy boots and trudge through the ubiquitous mud to the outhouse, which I find has been flooded by the downpour. After this business comes a search for fresh water—unsuccessful.

Back at the tent, David is washing his hands beneath the trickle from an old pump. The day has turned gray, but the storm has moved off. I wash my hands, grateful for this small mercy. Again, David helps me out of my boots and replaces them on fresh newspapers. Then he prepares dinner: a salmon salad, yogurt, wheat germ, and peaches.

So, here we are at the rally, the focus of this whole road trip for David, and all I can think about are the discomfort and inconvenience, and my fatigue. Resentment rises in me once again. I can feel my face has turned to stone. David takes note. "Ma, I'm sorry I got tied up."

I pounce. "Like you always do. You always need a crowd."

He's always been this way. After his first day at kinder-garten, I asked, "Did you make any new friends?"

"Yes, Ma," he replied happily. "Twenty-three: ten boys and thirteen girls."

After dinner I feel a little better. David now feels confi-dent that he can tell me, "Ma, I signed up to ride the new K1 BMW tomorrow at 7:30 A.M. We're talking 175 miles per hour! And don't start worrying—of course the class will be canceled if it's raining."

I silently pray for rain.

"Ma, are you all right?" he finally thinks to ask.

I'm not saying.

"Ma, I'm sorry. Forgive me?" He leans over and kisses me. I let him, even though at such close quarters it bothers me that he can see how age has taken its toll. Wasn't it only a few years ago I was climbing Canadian mountains with him?

Before she left him, David's ex-wife said he loved every-one else more than he loved her.

"Do you always have to do the David thing?" I ask irritably. "Helping anyone anywhere, even on the Hollywood Freeway. It could be a psychopath, a murderer. You don't use any judgment."

He doesn't answer, and my tirade fizzles out. He carefully stows our remaining provisions, steps outside, washes up, then returns to the tent.

I know what's on his mind. "Go," I say. I know he has people he wants to see.

"I won't go if you don't want me to."

"Remember, you have to get up early for that motorcycle ride."

"Don't worry, I will."

"Do they have to make those things go so fast?"

"It's fun, Ma."

"Go," I say, "have a good time." I really want him to.

"Don't wait up. There'll be a zydeco band. I may go. Just for a short while. Love you, Ma."

There is a flash of lightning before the flaps close behind him. I hear him stop to talk with Ben, who tells him his wife is going to town to do some shopping. I think of the cyclist who was killed by lightning. I hope that David will avoid standing under trees.

Then I feel too tired even to worry.

I am awakened by an angry female voice. "This is my vacation too, damn it! *You* watch the kids."

Teresa.

"Never enough money. All you're getting is a case of chronic bad breath. What I get from you I can get from any man."

"And you do," Ben strangles out the words. His voice is older than his looks.

I really don't want to hear this.

I am now reminded of a party in our basement many years ago. Leo and Amelia's husband, Hank, our doctor, were standing at the bar. Jeanne, the confirmed bachelorette, pushed in between them. She was petite and tight bodied, wore low-cut dresses and no bra. That night, when she leaned over the bar, her tanned breasts were almost fully exposed to view.

"She's laying her sex on the line," I said to Amelia.

Amelia turned her sharp blue eyes on me and said in her French accent, "I don't know what you're worried about. Hank is inept and Leo is indifferent."

I just laughed.

That night in bed Leo asked what I had found so funny. I told him. He put his arm around me and for a few minutes we stared out the window, up into the starless sky.

"You know," he finally said, "you and I really have something. We have each other."

The night I knew that Leo was dying, I came home from the hospital and hurled everything I could lay my hands on against the walls. So many people living unhappily with each other, why, God, did we, who loved our life together, have to be separated so soon?

That avalanche of rain I have been expecting has finally arrived. I turn on the flashlight. It's 1:30. I'm thinking I won't be able to sleep until David gets in when I hear the *putt-putt-putt* of the Dove as David walks her to her parking spot. I listen as, just outside, he removes his shoes before he enters without using a flashlight.

"David?"

"Ma? I hope you haven't been waiting up for me."

"No."

"The dance just broke up. I'm going to take a shower."

"Now?"

"I smell like a goat."

"It's the middle of the night, and it's so dark out there," I blurt out before I realize how ridiculous this would sound.

"You're not going to worry about that too," he counters gently.

"No. Of course not."

I don't fall asleep until he returns.

WEDNESDAY, JULY 18, RAPID CITY, SD

It's early morning on the eighteenth, officially the first day of the rally, and the ground throbs with the roar of what must be hundreds of motorcycles.

"You're not taking that class today, are you? David, it's so wet," I say to him right off as he opens, ties up the tent flaps. At least it has stopped raining.

"Look, Michael went with his wife to a motel last night. Since he may not get back in time, he asked me to take over his class on safe driving. I'll be gone a while."

"Does Michael know you got a hundred-dollar ticket for speeding on your way down to Los Angeles?"

"Not yet. Maybe I learned my lesson?"

"Maybe not. You called it a tax on enjoyment. I'd have more faith in your good sense if you called it a tax on stupidity."

"I think you should realize by now..." He has stopped

mid-sentence, aware of the futility. Now I realize what I've done. These may be the last words I will hear from him for the rest of the day. I want to kick myself. The chill is on, again.

It's frustrating trying to understand the enigma of my son. How articulately he can talk about pistons and crankshafts, books, music, the universe, but not his own feelings. It also seems he can entertain any opposing point of view—except mine, of course. If a girl tells him his best friend is putting him down, he says the man must have a reason.

"Sure," I said, "the reason is he wants her for himself."

Anything *I* say goes in one ear and out the other.

Once he said he was raised in a family of strong-minded individuals, and he was the youngest. Implication: we have crippled the independence of his judgment. But even if I could do it all over again, would I make the opposite mistake, of expressing no opinions whatsoever?

I begin to experience the same sickening feeling I had that night in Santa Fe. It occurs to me now: David wasn't inviting his mother to the rally when he asked me. He invited a friend, and instead, his mother came along.

We sit in silence for the longest time, still no sign at all of the sun this morning. I stare out the tent at the mire of mud. *All right, so my son is an enigma. Then what of this woman I'm not at all sure I like, who often talks too much and out of turn, whose opinions must always be so scathing?*

I came on this trip with hopes of mending a growing rift with my son. But more than that, to find that better, stronger, braver me—shedding my dry and brittle faults like a snake does its worn-out skin. But anger and grief won't be shaken off so easily. That resentful old woman I thought I left behind in Los Angeles has never really left my side.

David has offered me a bowl of bran flakes with the milk I thought would have soured by now. It hasn't. I haven't even said good morning to him yet. Now I say almost defiantly, "I think I'll go with you to that dance tonight."

He frowns. "It's a zydeco band, Ma."

"So what? No illusions this time. Or would I be cramping your style?"

"It's not that, Ma. It's just that the music will be loud. And there'll probably be some pot smoking."

"Fine. Maybe that's what I need—medical marijuana."

"Ma…"

"Well, I'd rather tag along with you than brood here in this tent." He sets down his bowl. "You going to Michael's class now?"

He nods.

"Mind if I walk along with you part of the way?"

"'Course not, Ma."

Along the way he stops at a tree. On one of its twigs is something green and luminescent. "It's a praying mantis. She'll eat anything smaller than herself. Adult mantises will sometimes eat each other. They'll even eat hummingbirds."

When we come to a clearing where the trees have been cut, David tells me to sit on a stump. He kneels and ties my shoelaces, a reversal of roles I don't even want to think about. "Can't have you tripping and falling, Ma."

There is an aroma of bacon and eggs in the air. Suddenly, the rain begins to fall in a frenzy. Before we separate, David suggests I go back and get my rain suit.

"Have a good day," I say and try to mean it.

Sometimes when I'm with my son, I feel like a barnacle clinging to the hull of a clipper ship.

An announcement crackles over the PA system: We are all encouraged to congregate at the beer garden. Great—standing bunched up shoulder to shoulder, all very cozy, like Tokyo subway commuters packed into their morning sardine cans. Pass.

Most of the classes have been canceled due to sporadic rain, including the one for passengers, which David had wanted me to attend. It's a relief; with my luck I would have found myself among a bunch of bikini girls with X-ray eyes, staring right through my worsted knickers to the safety pin that holds up my panties with their worn-out elastic waistband. Why must I compare myself to twenty-year-olds?

Still, the air smells clean. There is a certain austere beauty about the day: the trees appear glazed, the grass iridescent. The morning's sudden charm dissipates with my arrival back at the British Columbia section, with its muddy path, its two portable potties, the worms, ants, mosquitoes out in force, defying the weather. Even the birds appear miserably drenched. I won't be able to sketch Ben's children today.

Back in the tent, I feel out of sorts. It's too dark to read, so I open the flap and sit looking out. The rain starts up again. I'm brooding again. What are we all, in the final analysis? Just networks of nerves, arteries, veins, vital organs?

Looking up at the heavens together at night, Leo would say, "How infinitesimal we really are."

An envoy from the realm of faerie has intervened and the rain has been called off. I put my boots back on and go looking for the corral.

Outside the gates to the park, I follow the horse path. I can hear the tremulous neighs of the horses. With the natural love of a kindred spirit, I love horses just for their sensitivity.

Papa was a jockey, briefly. "What kind of job is that for a nice Jewish husband?" my maternal grandmother complained, so Papa quit and worked at odd jobs. He never made any money, and he never again heard the hurrahs of the cheering crowd.

I have found the corral and the horses. They are proud creatures who tolerate us against their better judgment. I have brought along my rain-blistered sketchpad, pencils, and charcoal. I sit on a stump and begin to sketch. Away from the fairgrounds, here in the quiet, I can begin to relax. The knot in my throat begins to loosen.

My concentration is broken by the high-pitched laughter of a girl. Some distance away, but still within sight, a couple are nuzzling. It seems they have come from the rally, looking for privacy. The boy is longhaired and blond. The girl's hair clings wetly to her head. As his mouth moves wolfishly from one bared nipple to the other, she throws her head back, the pink tip of her tongue thrust visibly from her gaping mouth.

When his hand reaches for the zipper of her jeans, I hastily move off—shock or embarrassment driving me away? In my day, a woman's joy in carnal pleasure was equated with promiscuity. I never dared to be forward, even with men I really admired. I wonder now if platonic love and repression share a common source. What of the pure love I seek from my son? Maybe Freud was right. Can anyone really be sure of love's source?

Maybe the children will be out now.

On my way back I pass a lovely young woman on horseback, riding toward the corral. She flashes me an innocent smile.

The sun appears, finally. This makes me realize how I miss being on the Dove. I even enjoy the speed, but I must never tell David that. I heard Mark ask him during our stopover, "Do you go slower when Mom's on the back?"

"No, I like pushing her limits," replied David with a diabolical grin.

More like pushing my buttons.

Back at camp, I was right: the children have come out with the sun and are playing in the sidecars. I can sketch them if they'd like. I ask their permission. They agree and I start with the five-year-old, who sticks his thumbs in his ears. "Like this," he insists.

"Behave! And sit still," commands the seven-year-old.

And he does to my surprise, for longer than I expect. As I sketch, using charcoal because it's faster, I feel good. The shutters on my thoughts open up to the sunshine. I do the older one in pencil. They are beautiful, these two boys—Norman Rockwell children: freckled faces, wide blue eyes, heavy dark lashes, pug noses.

Ben comes out to watch, bringing with him some pressed apricot candy, which pleases the boys but gums up my damned partials and makes me lisp. Once I had a voice, now just a cracked excuse of a voice. And then there are the hated partials, complicating speech further. It seems time just wants to shut me up.

When the boys have grown tired of sitting, I let them go. With a yelp, the Indians run off to fight the palefaces. (Children can be refreshingly politically incorrect.) Getting these two portraits has been a delight. I carefully tear the sketches away from the pad and offer them to Ben, who is delighted to accept.

We fall into talk about David. "From age twelve," I tell Ben, "he was fixing everyone's car on the block. Everyone's but mine.

"'Can't help it,' David would say. 'I just got a block about fixing yours, Ma.'

"Now and then my husband, Leo, would intervene and tell David to fix it. Then usually he would. But once Leo had to tell him, 'Do it today.'

"'I'll do it when I have time,' David said.

"'You've got nothing but time,' Leo said to him. Leo

knew what he was talking about; he had only a few more months to live."

"I'm sorry," Ben says.

"Anyway, I was sure this time the car would be fixed, but when Leo and I returned from our walk, we found he still hadn't done it. This time I was angry. I told David very solemnly, 'I meant never to tell you this, but, David … you were adopted.'

"David threw his arms into the air and cried out, 'Thank God!'

"'Where you going?' I asked him as he started across the street.

"'To break the good news to Tim.'

"So much for my efforts to punish him. That was the first time I heard Leo laugh since his stroke. How much Leo has missed not knowing his grown sons. How much they have missed not knowing their not-quite-grown father."

Ben smiles at the anecdote. "People really respect David up in Vernon. He has a reputation for honesty and skill."

"The first time I visited David in the mountains, his pants were crisscrossed with patches. At home, he'd always worn designer jeans. 'You need a new pair of pants,' I told him, looking at a rip in one of the knees.

"'No, Ma,' he said, 'I need another patch.'

"He'd changed," I tell Ben. "He'd found himself."

It was cold there, even in late August. I watched David cut the trees to build his house, and I was proud of my city-bred son, living in that old shack, surrounded by nothing but wilderness, the outhouse, animal carcasses, and the rusty old bathtub catching the rain.

"It took him years, but he finally built a wonderful house," Ben says. "Well designed, compact, unpretentious."

I have dropped my charcoal. Ben picks it up from the mud and gallantly wipes it off before he hands it back. His eyes are direct and blue.

Teresa comes out of their tent and barely acknowledges my presence with a nod. My throat constricts with distaste as I remember Ben's words, "And you do." She mounts her bike and with a casual wave she's off.

Ben waves back just as casually, but his Adam's apple is working. "She does this all the time. Leaves me with the kids. I guess I must love her, or I wouldn't put up with it."

An awkward silence follows before I think to ask, "Am I keeping you?"

"No, I'm glad for the company."

Michael and his wife drop by now to ask Ben to join them for dinner in town.

"Can't. I don't know when my wife'll be back."

When they have gone, I hand Ben the sketch I have been doing as we speak. The likeness makes him look older than he really is, wise, and rather sad.

"You catch people from the inside out, don't you?" he says, smiling ruefully. "I wish everyone could see me that clearly."

"Maybe she does. She knows you'll always be a good father. She must love you for that."

There's a brief silence, broken only by the distant revs of motorcycles and a screeching PA announcement. Ben pats my hand lightly with his. "David tells me you're planning to go to Yellowstone. There's an absolutely wonderful scenic road off Highway 14 and Alternate 14. I've got to tell him about it."

"Is it dangerous? If it is, that's the road he'll want to take."

Ben's eyes twinkle. "We're mountain people. Mountain people don't think of mountains as dangerous."

"Are you going to the rally awards ceremony tomorrow evening?" I ask him.

"No reason to go," he says.

"That doesn't stop David. We've come well over four thousand miles, probably farther than anyone else. But I understand those awards go to people who've come from overseas. Is that fair? They didn't fly here on their bikes."

Ben agrees that it's unfair.

It's time I excused myself to go rest up for tonight's dance. I gather up my sketchbook and charcoal.

"Thank you," Ben says, and gives me a quick hug.

As I walk back to the tent for a nap, I think about this morning's events. It seems that David is the spirit of Gandhi with everyone but me. It must be my fault that we don't get along better.

I've been living large on this trip. I'm not accustomed to the extremes—both the highs and lows. So if I find myself at times feeling exhausted and emotionally fragile, then I must learn to accept that. I must also accept my near invisibility among these raucous, beer-swilling men and women half my age, even though sometimes it makes me feel like throwing a fit. I must learn to appreciate this challenge to my narrow everyday existence—with which I have grown much too comfortable—with its compromise exchange of my spent youth for those treasured memories: the candlelit winter nights, lovely musical evenings with Leo and friends, the engaging talk, playing my one-hundred-year-old pipe organ. That music is in my heart still. I'm still alive, still hungry for adventure. And here it is all around me.

My eyes flutter back open when I hear the voices of two Canadian latecomers. One says, "Let Quebec secede, if she wants to. It won't make any difference to us."

No, I don't suppose it will, I think to myself as I close my eyes again.

When I wake, it's dark. I hear the *putt-putt* of the Dove. I am anticipating the bit of adventure that David's presence always promises.

As he changes into the red plaid shirt I like so much on him, he tells me, "Ma, tomorrow we'll check out the warehouse, maybe find a helmet for you. Some of the stands may still be open. Should we get something to eat?"

I don't bother changing. I put on some lipstick. It's a motorcycle rally, not a ball.

As we approach the stalls, the smell of hot dogs and French fries brings back memories like an old melody: Leo waking me at 2:00 A.M., to take me to Coney Island for hot dogs at Nathan's. Leo was always good for the unexpected. Whatever we did together, it was always fun.

"What should I have?" I wonder out loud. "A hot dog, patty melt, ice cream?"

"Actually, I was thinking of veggie burgers and steamed vegetables."

Spoilsport.

We go to a stand that serves oriental food. David asks for some steamed vegetables. The price is double everything else on the menu. "He's charging you too much, David," I have to say.

"It's my money, Ma."

"You said you were running out."

"It's only money. Isn't that what you and Leo used to say? When did you get so concerned about money."

I am about to retort, That's why we never had any! But was that really true? There was always enough for camps, family vacations, concerts, the occasional theater tickets. Just not enough for savings.

I can hear the zydeco band warming up. Everything is lit up.

We meet up with the sullen motorcyclist we met earlier at Mount Rushmore, now tinkering with his upended motorcycle.

"Will you take a look at my bike?" he says, looking at us with his ice-blue, fishy eyes, already handing David a wrench. He makes it sound like an order. Even though David is wearing his nice plaid shirt, he doesn't hesitate. He squats abruptly beside the bike, as if he were doing a Polish dance, and immediately his hands go to his back. He straightens up for a moment, clearly in pain. Still, he returns to work and soon has the problem fixed.

"Thanks, man," grunts Fishy.

"Hey, would you mind taking a look at mine?" says a young woman leaning on her parked cycle.

Never refuse a lady in distress.

We finally reach the beer garden. We sit down at a folding table and begin sipping our brown ales, watching the dancers. It's mostly men without partners, wheeling and waving their arms wildly, as if they were on peyote. (Maybe they are.) One of the few girls among them is serially groped. Were these boys never weaned?

I suppose David would prefer to be here with someone younger and prettier—someone not his mother, anyway. I *was* young myself once. And wicked. Sometimes I deliberately brought pretty women to the house, just to gauge Leo's reaction. He loved the good conversation of intelligent women. But there was never a hint of straying.

Maybe once there was a gleam in his eye. I confronted him about it.

"I'm not dead, only married," he winked. Then he tilted my chin up and said very seriously, "You're my woman, and you're enough trouble for any man."

"Till death do us part?" I asked.

"Till death do us part," he answered, kissing me.

David talks for a while with a girl who keeps running her

tongue over her top lip. Then he thinks to ask me to dance. I follow him out on the floor and try to move to the erratic and unfamiliar music, but my Nikes seem to stick to the floor. There's nothing very musical about it, really, just so much noise, and the dancing nothing but masturbatory gyrations and a great deal of sweating.

The music stops and I excuse myself. "I think I'll go for a walk, check up on the moon." Again, I'm a ship out of her own waters.

"All right, Ma, but take the flashlight. Be careful of the scrub brush and stumps. And check in with me in an hour. I won't stay long."

Down the path lies a pretty grove of trees. I have never gotten over the splendor of trees: *Poems are made by fools like me...* The other kids in class pointed at me and giggled when I recited Kilmer's "Trees."

Twice I stumble and nearly fall. A bearlike shadow is a man urinating against a tree. He turns and stares at me blankly, swaying. "A little more decorum would be welcome," I mutter to myself, turning quickly back toward the beer garden where a group of men have gathered beneath an awning with their beer and an assortment of pipes. The smoke hangs thick in the air.

I sit at a distance, but close enough to hear. They talk about the rain, how their wives won't ride in it. Some of them, who would have come along, didn't because of the "vile" weather. Even the men confess they don't like riding in the rain and dark. I feel vindicated.

The moon glows between the stony mountains; the stars

peep down. I remember how I used to cut them out of construction paper in school.

The changing scenery, the unfamiliar situations—this is undoubtedly what has stimulated the rush of memories. Staring up at the sky, I think of my school days. I see myself standing in a corner, punished for being a "dunce." My first-grade teacher placed me in the back row, then stood me in the corner for being inattentive. She forgot about me, and there I stood for what seemed like hours. I was wetting myself and crying, because I was ashamed to tell her I hadn't been able to see the blackboard. To this day, the memory of the perfume she wore still nauseates me.

When there is a lull in the music, I go back to the dance. David is again talking to the girl with the reptilian tongue. When he sees me, he surprises me by extricating himself immediately with a wave.

On our way out, I say something I have been wanting to say for a long time. "You know, Rachel's been in Africa for a whole year. She may have met another man."

No response.

"You were too ready to move Barbie in," I go on. "If you had shown any interest in Rachel, she would never have left Vernon."

"I wrote her as soon as Barbie left, Ma. I couldn't do that while there was still a chance things would work out with Barbie. I couldn't hurt Rachel like that."

I remember bitterly how he had hurt me for Barbie, but I drop the subject. We walk in silence, only the sounds of twigs breaking underfoot and the gossip of the crickets. If I keep quiet, I think to myself, maybe he will talk, really talk.

As usual, my resolution is short-lived. When we reach the tent, David announces, "I'm riding into town with some of the guys."

Back at the dance I heard a man say, preceded by a loud belch from his barrel chest, "I know where I can get some good weed." The she-devil in me surfaces. "What for?" I ask. "To smoke pot?"

David sighs, turns, and walks off.

I lie awake, worrying about my grown son.

THURSDAY, JULY 19, RAPID CITY, SD

David already has breakfast ready when I wake: yogurt, wheat germ, bananas, but no coffee. This morning I long for the aroma of freshly ground coffee.

"I heard over the loudspeaker they need mechanics. They said they would pay well," I inform him, trying to strike up conversation.

"I don't want to be paid. I don't want the obligation."

Just like David.

He tells me he is going to take the K1 out again this morning for an hour. "When I get back, we'll go to the warehouse to look for a helmet. We'll eat at the cafeteria tonight. I hear the food is pretty good."

It seems that elusive intimacy between us has evaporated once again. This will be our last full day at the rally, and with David running around doing free repair jobs, there won't be much time for us to make up.

Again, I walk part of the way with him to his class. He is trying to conserve gas until we leave. Later today he will check the Dove over thoroughly to make sure she is up to the rest of the trip.

Along the way, we meet up with a striking man I had noticed earlier. He might almost be considered attractive, except that every visible square inch of him is tattooed, except his face. "Hey, Frank," David smiles in greeting and introduces us.

At some point in the conversation, I can't resist saying, "When *I* was a young girl, even one tattoo would have turned me off."

Frank shrugs, laughing. "You don't know the half of it, lady. Guess I *could* have them removed, just for you, but it would be very painful."

When we walk on, I can't help looking back. The tattooed man grins and blows me a kiss.

I tell David I think I'll head back to the tent for a nap and he only nods. No little kiss when he goes off to his class, so I know he is still upset with me for last night.

My nap has turned into a long sleep. It is late afternoon when I wake. David is working on the Dove. "Ma," he says, "that K1 is the smoothest, sweetest thing on the road."

"Thinking of trading in the Dove?"

"The Dove? Never! No, I'm satisfied with my faithful old friend here. Besides, she handles much better at low speeds."

What low speeds?!

The day has turned out fine. I spread the sheepskin on the dry grass and sit, dividing my attention between David and Ben's children, who are playing catch. I remember myself at their age, playing ball, skipping rope, hoping Papa would take me out for a walk in the evening.

When David has finished his inspection and routine maintenance, we wash our hands and go back into the tent for something to eat. It's still a long time before dinner.

"Did you teach the safe riding class again for Michael?" I ask.

"As a matter of fact, I did."

"I hope you plan to take your own advice the next time you get on one of those K1s. What's the point of having motorcycles that go faster than the legal speed limit, anyway?"

"I told you, because it's fun. You're repeating yourself, Ma." He is cutting up a cantaloupe with his pocketknife. "I hope it's good."

"Smell it," I tell him. "If it's got a fruity smell, it's good and ripe. I didn't know you bought a cantaloupe."

"Bought it at a market in town that stays open late for the rally people. Last night, when I was supposed to be out smoking pot." David smells the cantaloupe and smiles. "Smells good," he pronounces, then holds it out. "Wanna smell it?"

We look at each other for several moments before I say, "No, I trust your judgment."

As we walk toward the warehouse, everyone seems to know David. There are lots of hellos, lots of expressions of gratitude, the women not least of all—good-looking girls, naturally, scantily clad in bikini tops.

"Pretty," I remark, ambiguously.

David arches an eyebrow.

A little dog, the first I have seen here, moves through the crowd, sniffing, seemingly searching for something—or someone. It seems to be lost. Poor little dog. It belongs here about as much as I do.

Our path slopes gently downward, and David reaches out to take my hand.

The warehouse is crowded and noisy. There are tables piled with T-shirts, goggles, leather jackets, leather gloves, tools, pins, placards, postcards. Everyone is buying.

"Hey, David! Any special brand of motor lubricant?" someone yells out over the heads of the crowd.

"Buy the cheapest," he yells back. "They all perform the same."

He turns to me and says, "You know I could use a credit card to get you a better helmet. They'll take it here."

"For two hundred dollars? Absolutely not. I can live with the one I have for the rest of the trip. I'll get one later at a garage sale."

"You have to be careful, though, Ma. If it's nicked or scratched, it may have been in an accident."

Now a man with a long jaw and bullfrog voice calls out, "David, that K1 was quite an experience this morning. Those things go too damn fast! I couldn't control the speed."

I like him instantly for this.

"They do take some getting used to," David admits.

Later, at the cafeteria, David leaves me at an outside table and goes in for the food. He comes out juggling two trays: hot beans, baked flounder, peas and carrots, hot rolls, and tea.

When we finish eating, he tells me to show him my boots. "I bought some material to cover the pedals so you won't burn your ankles." He removes my boots and cuts away the burnt sections of the rubber heels.

"I hope you won't have time for any more K1 racing," I tell him as he works.

"Why do you insist on imagining all kinds of disasters? I'm not looking for danger, Ma. I just want to enjoy my life to the fullest. Stop trying to make a mama's boy out of me."

Barbie had given me the same advice. Funny she should say that to me, since *she* had David trained like Pavlov's dog.

I remember something Mark told me: "Stop trying to impose your will on David. He's making a big investment of time in you. I could never do for you what he's doing."

"He could be composing music for me instead," I retort.

"He can do that too, when he's ready."

"Still."

"Ma, where would the rest of us be without the Davids of this world?" Mark had asked.

I wish I understood the chemistry that makes me so much

less anxious about Mark. When he says, "Ma, I heard you," I know he means it.

Still, David does show more restraint toward me than I did toward my mother. I remember how Leo would come home and find me on the phone, stamping my foot in rage.

"Talking with your mother?" he would smile.

Mark says that David has "the clarity of the creative mind to envision what things can be."

My own mental exercises must seem feeble by comparison.

"David, I'm sorry," I tell him now.

He looks surprised, then pleased. "Going with me to the awards ceremony tonight?"

"No," I say, my feelings wounded. If only he had asked me to come because he really wanted me along.

I lie on the mattress in our tent, brooding. Yes, I'm tired, but of course I would have liked to attend the ceremony, if not for my silly pride. At least I would be spending the evening with David.

I must have dropped off to sleep. I'm awakened with a start as the award announcements begin to blast from the loudspeakers.

"The award for the most mileage..." does not go to David, despite those four thousand miles he's logged since British Columbia.

There is an award for the oldest rider, an eighty-year-old man. More power to him.

Then to my utter horror, I hear my own name announced. I sit bolt upright.

"Sixty-eight years, four months, one week, three days," intones a voice like God's.

I am receiving an award for being the oldest passenger.

An ovation rises from the neighboring tents. Ben's head pokes through our tent opening. "Did you hear that?" he asks.

The adrenaline is pumping through my system. "Yes, I heard—loud and clear. I just got the booby prize!"

Ben is chivalrous. "Hey, I took you for at least ten years younger. You're still an attractive lady, you know. I mean, for someone your age."

"Thanks a bunch."

"I wish you many more birthdays," Ben says before he wisely ducks back out.

He can wish them, but it doesn't mean they will come. Or that they are especially welcome.

When David returns, bursting into the tent and full of excitement, I have recovered my equanimity; I feign senility. "Ma, did you hear? You won an award!"

"What's that you say, sonny?"

"Ma," he bubbles, showing me, "you got a plaque."

"Plaque? Arterial plaque?"

"What do you want me to do with it?"

"You know what you can do with it," I tell him, dropping the act.

"Ah, come on!"

"You forgot the seven hours. I was born at three in the afternoon."

"I'm proud of you, Ma."

"David, why didn't you just have Peter Jennings announce it on the evening news?"

"Awwww, Ma! Be a sport."

Seven thousand five hundred people heard that announcement. After all these years of hiding my age because I am widowed, because there is no greater mortal shame in this world, it seems, than being a woman growing old all alone, my secret is out.

Homecoming

FRIDAY, JULY 20, DEVILS TOWER, WY

It's looking like rain again for our return to the road.

David says his few good-byes. I find I'm sad to be leaving Ben. The one who should love him most seems to appreciate him least. This makes me think guiltily of David, as I watch him, with tears in my eyes, hugging friends and patting shoulders.

The rally is behind us. To my surprise, I am feeling a certain tenderness toward him, and a strange sense of relief: All these years of lying about my age, and hating it, and now I don't feel like I have to lie anymore.

David stops on our way out of town for gas. Parked under cover of a tree—a light rain has begun to fall, almost reluctantly, before the wind picks up—he plugs his electric shaver into an outlet on the bike and shaves while he studies the map. "We'll be making a side trip to Badlands National

Park, then we'll backtrack. We should still make Devils Tower before dark."

Fifty miles later, David points to a rest area with a table, a bench, one tree, and a privy. We stop for our seven-grain bread, Swiss cheese, and mustard with a pickle, and apple juice.

When we finish eating, David says, "Put your foot up on the bench and I'll massage your knee."

When it's my turn, I punch his spine up and down almost gleefully. Hitting him today is a pleasure. I must still be smarting from last night's revelation.

The Badlands is a nightmarish place, all sand, fossilized rock, and clay spires—a huge desolate dumping ground for all the sorrows of those who have passed through them. They frighten me. We don't stay long.

"I didn't know nature could be so ugly," I groan over the intercom, once we're back on the highway.

"Ugly? I don't know. I'd say more like a certain grandeur." David looks up at the sky. "Weather's changing again, Ma. There's spit in the air."

David suggests we stop and get into our rain suits. I look up at the blue-jawed sky as it begins to mist over. "Forget the suits, David. Let's just get of here."

"Okay, but we're going to have to go back the way we came."

I groan again, counting to ten, telling myself it can't be helped. I begin to sing, *"This land is your land, this land is my land..."*

David has picked up the melody. *"This land is good land, this land is bad land…"*

He's rubbing my knee now, pleased that I'm singing and happy again.

Eventually, we ride out of the park, and onto the main highway where I'm cheered by the sight of green trees and the wet rich smell of vegetation. Soon we spot a billboard, the first of many, aggressively promoting the legend of Wall Drug.

One version goes like this: More than a hundred years ago, a prospector by the name of Wall discovered a clear, crystal stream. He had the good sense to stop and build a general store. Later he added a tavern. He started leaving handbills wherever prospectors would find them, advertising free springwater. I could just see them, dirt-caked, ragged, crawling into town on their bellies, crawling for the free springwater and their very lives. The town that grew up around the store became Wall, South Dakota.

At last we stand in front of the celebrated Wall Drug. Actually, it's now more of a mini-mall than a drugstore—a sprawling, magnificent tourist trap. Times certainly have changed: no prospectors crawling on their bellies, just a horde of summer-vacation pioneers hauling their broods through the New West in station wagons. I'm reluctant to go in.

"Come on, Ma. This place is world famous. We won't stay long."

At the entrance stand larger-than-life prospectors carved in wood. Their women, wearing bonnets and pinafores, sit on benches, apparently taking a break from their allemandes. "Take One," a sign coyly invites, and David takes a few shots of me, hamming it up, with my arms around one of the giant prospectors.

I follow David inside, toward the music coming from a miniature wood-and-steel orchestra, tiny toy musicians playing the heart-wrenching "Kiss Me Again." The store smells of perfume, soap, fruit, pies, hot bread, and coffee.

We are sauntering down an aisle when up walks Stan, another cyclist from the rally. Stan's girlfriend, Mindy, appears to be about thirteen. When she sees David, this Lolita tosses her long black tresses over her shoulder and ogles him.

Mindy tells us how her grandfather owns a general store with a huge dance hall behind it in a neighboring state. On Saturdays she waitresses. "Sometimes old men come in and listen to those old songs," she says. "They cry. It's disgusting." She is holding her cute little nose between thumb and index finger. "They make me want to puke."

"Why? They're classics, aren't they?" I ask her deliberately.

"Classics?" Either the word means nothing to her, or she wants to puke again.

As we leave the store, we see a woman restraining a larger, older boy and telling a smaller one, hers evidently, "Hit him! Go on, hit him back!"

At this moment another woman, the mother of the older boy presumably, arrives with blazing eyes, and the women start screaming at each other.

"Shall we stay and watch *them* have a go at it?" I ask.

"Let's not and say we did." David smiles, revealing his dimple. ·

We're riding through the mountains once more, the landscape is green and lush. The smell of pine is exciting. "You know, they say a single mouse can gnaw a pine to death," David informs me over the intercom. I ponder that for a few miles.

I gorge myself on the scenery as we enter Devils Tower National Monument, in the northeast corner of Wyoming, just below the Montana border. David pulls up alongside several other BMWs and stops. The setting is ideal. I have my son all to myself again, a few more minutes for that jug of a perfect twenty-four hours. Time is really the greatest treasure. For now, I'm a very rich woman.

Making sure he can see I'm smiling, I say, "David, I believe you were flirting with Little Mindy the musicologist. Isn't she jailbait?"

"Don't worry, Ma. Not my type."

We take pictures of each other with the tower in the background. "The legend claims that two women were being chased by bears. To escape, they climbed the tower. The bears clambered up after them as they climbed and climbed and the tower grew and grew. The bears gave up, leaving their claw marks behind on the sides of the tower. The women were never seen again."

I can tell by his voice that David has something on his mind.

We have been spotted by a group of six or seven cyclists who have staked out a lovely campsite inside the park. Plenty of room and food—we are welcome to join them. David sets up our tent. There is a roaring fire and a heap of wood to feed it.

We eat the good and healthful foods David insists upon, rich in vitamins and minerals, while around us the other campers feast on frankfurters, marshmallows, and beer. I envy them.

After we eat and shower, I say good night to the group gathered about the fire and slip into the tent. David follows. "Why don't you join us?"

"And put a damper on the fun? No, thank you."

He doesn't insist. "I'll leave the tent flap open so you can see the fire."

The fireside conversation falls short of profound. The gist of it: they wish they had some women along with them. They are a scruffy bunch who could pass for a police lineup. The one with the loudest voice is boasting, "Thought I'd have a blast with the blonde with the big tits. Silicone, like rocks, like taking a cold-water shower when you expected hot."

I turn my attention to the night sky. I wish I could reach up and grab a star. God wouldn't miss just one. The smell of the burning wood is entrancing, and I feel myself drifting off.

SATURDAY, JULY 21, CODY, WY

I am roused by the sounds of the men stamping out what is

left of the fire. They say their hearty good-byes. David deals out some of his hugging bear T-shirts (his business logo)— "if you should ever happen to come to Canada."

After the others have left, I emerge from the tent and stretch my arms in the crisp morning air. "Morning!" David calls as he begins loading the Dove. "Good thing you didn't join us. Those guys had all eaten lunch at a place called The Beanery, and they were breaking wind all night at seventy miles an hour."

Charming.

Our next destintion is Yellowstone and Highway 14. We're tooling down Alternate Highway 14 beyond Sheridan, and I have never felt so close to heaven. The Sioux believed in the Great Spirit in the sky, and the sky here could make me a believer myself.

David pulls onto the shoulder in a high pass. Below are twin peaks lush with blue spruce. "Just look at the view, Ma." He makes a wide arc with his arm across the silver-blue sky.

David has such reverence for nature. Well, he *was* conceived during a trip to the Catskills, as I recall, smiling to myself.

The evening sun has paled, then dropped behind the trees. In Cody we stop at a supermarket. After I use the rest room, I lead David through the frozen food section. Maybe he'll relent and buy something to eat that has some flavor for a change.

My hopes are dashed. We sit down to familiar fare: yogurt

and salmon, wheat bread, and oranges. David asks me if I'm tired.

I grunt out a laugh. "Who, me, tired? Take me to the highest mountain and let me climb." I may drop dead of heart failure after the first ten feet. But no, surprisingly, I'm not particularly tired.

My mind travels back to the previous night. "David, those men at Devils Tower, they talked about women like they're not people, just some sort of necessary commodity. Men like that infuriate me. I went to a lecture once, given by a radio talk-show host touting his new book. The audience was mostly women who listened to his show religiously."

David doesn't seem to be listening. Something seems to be troubling him again, ever since Devils Tower. He just looks down at his hands while I continue. "See, this guy's wearing a phony beard, mustache, a hairpiece. He asks the audience, 'Have you ladies been using your vibrators lately?'"

David looks up.

"Are you listening?" I ask him.

"Sorry," he says.

I go on with my story. "He starts calling for questions. He calls on me first. He's already in trouble and this is his last mistake. 'You're a *radio* talk-show host. What's with the disguise?' And he says, 'Touché.' And I say, 'No, toupee.' Everyone laughed."

David fixes me with his gaze before he says, "Ma, that's what I like about you. You say the things other people think but would never have the nerve to say."

Anything he likes about me is encouraging. A longish silence follows before I finally ask, "David, what is it?"

He looks at me guiltily. "Barbie's meeting us in Yellowstone."

My mouth runs dry, my heart begins to pound. "David, why? I thought this trip was for *us*. You know how I feel about her!"

The dove of peace has spread its wings and disappeared over the horizon.

Two years ago, David urged me to come stay with him in Vernon. "Ma," he said on the phone, "I know you love the land same as I do. I want you to think about moving up here. Come spend a month at least and try it out. There's so much going on: painting, writing groups, theater. I think you'd be happy here. And you'll breathe some good air for a change."

During the flight to Kelowna, the nearest airport to Vernon, a fierce electrical storm sent the sixteen passengers on the plane spinning against each other; the pilot had to turn back. We finally made it to Kelowna, three hours late. David enfolded me in his arms. "Thank God, you're safe!"

Not quite. The storm was a portent.

As we left the airport, with his arm still around my shoulders, he told me, "We're going to Barbie's place first, down in town. I've been staying there all week. I made a fire before I left, Ma. She never used the fireplace so it took some time to get it started. I told her my mother likes nothing better than a roaring fire."

We fell silent as I digested this second unexpected turn of events. Finally, I said, "So what's she like?"

His brow wrinkled. "Well, she's honest and direct like you. She doesn't care much about books or music, but she's interested in me. She makes me talk about my feelings. She's always asking me questions."

Funny. He never seemed very enthusiastic about my questions. "Do you think she's the right one for you?" I asked him.

There was a long pause before he replied, "I'm not sure."

He drove in silence for a while, one hand on the wheel, the other on mine. Then, nervously, he tells me, "Ma, I rented a small bungalow for you, right next to my shop. I rented it for a month."

"I don't understand."

"Barbie is moving in with me tomorrow."

The news stunned me, of course. "David, I thought I was going to spend time with you up at the house."

"Of course, Ma, I want you to spend time with us."

I hadn't planned on the "us."

He burbled on. "Barbie's been great, Ma. I asked her to take care of the things I didn't have time to do. She brought down linens, dishes, the old record player you gave me, and some records. I was going to rent a place for you after you got here, but Barbie said she was a little uncomfortable about your being in the house with her before she got … well, you know … acclimated."

I was hurt. Who wouldn't have been? I tried not to show

it. Instead I needled him. "Well, it's nice to know at least your male hormones are working."

End of conversation. His hand slipped away.

The rain had stopped. We drove into Vernon, with its clean streets lined with brick homes. The air was cool, even for a British Columbia summer. A little way up the mountain, we stopped at a cluster of small rental houses. Barbie—a tall, skinny, nondescript blonde—met us at the door. *No doll, this one,* I thought.

The house was starkly furnished: no pictures, plants, or books. But then she was moving, I reminded myself.

I hadn't brought her a gift, of course, so I took off my coral necklace. "Here. I'm sorry I didn't have time to go shopping. I'd like you to have this."

"I never wear those things," she said flatly. "But it'll look pretty hanging in our bedroom window."

David put on water to boil for spaghetti. "I cooked the sauce for three hours yesterday the way you used to do it, Ma."

"David does the cooking. I don't like it myself," Barbie announced. "I'm not domesticated, and nobody is *going* to domesticate me."

Bully for you.

I thought of David's long hours at work and of him coming home late in the evening to cook for this tough young cookie who had learned to look out only for Number One. Couldn't he find a woman with a figure? I wondered.

David answered one of my unspoken questions. "We eat dinner out most evenings. You'll join us, I hope, Ma."

"Us" again. For this I flew through a lightning storm?

While we were eating, David told me, "I'm going to take you to the Cultural Arts Center and introduce you to the director. He'll see that you meet people. You'll love living up here, Ma."

"So where are you proposing that I live?"

His eyes lit up. "Of course, I'll get that house built for you on the spot I promised. You'll have a southern exposure. You can paint again. You've gotta spend winter up here, Ma. Winter is the loveliest season. The cold is dry. The sight of the snow on the mountains is breathtaking. You'll love the cross-country skiing."

The spot reserved for my new home was in a lovely shaded glen on David's property. Here between two huge trees David had strung up a green hammock he bought in Mexico. I loved to read there. David would come with his cat and sit stroking it while we talked. Nearby, he had installed a swing just for me. He used to push me in it. Sometimes I would stand up on the seat, flying high, and look down at the bluest of blue lakes. In the late afternoons, the shadows would come stealing in, trailing gold, and I would think how full my life had become.

This was exactly the home that I, child of the slums, once dreamed of having.

"I'm going to Quebec for a month this winter. You can come visit then," Barbie allowed.

That first night in Vernon, I slept on Barbie's old sofa. In the morning David took me on my first motorcycle ride of the season. We rode down to the bungalow he had rented for me. It was shabby and sparely furnished. The springs in the mattress creaked; the mattress itself looked none too sanitary.

We sat a while and talked. "I'm not in love with Barbie," David confessed, "but I'm learning to love her. She's never too busy to listen to me."

This explanation ill concealed an accusation: *I* was always too busy, it seems.

"This place is convenient," David said, meaning the bungalow. "I can spend my free time with you. When I have any."

"I can come and visit you too," I offered, but my heart was sinking.

He brought my things in and helped me unpack. He showed me how he had stocked the refrigerator with wheat germ, yogurt, fruit, bread, milk, juice, and cereals.

When he left, I just stood looking out the window at the neatly kept lot for sale across the street. The bungalow was on a quiet block in a residential district. David's shop was the only business.

I took inventory of my new digs. There were some familiar dishes in the cupboard. After all, David did need a woman up there on the mountain. Still, he thanked her much too profusely for clearing the dishes from the table; it was the first helpful thing I had seen her do.

I started to make the double bed, but there were only two single sheets, both stained; David had never owned a single bed. There was only one torn towel and one blanket so thin that holes had begun to appear. What had happened to all the nice linen, the many warm blankets I had given him over the years?

I sat down heavily on the bed, staring into space. It looked as if I would have to sleep on the bare mattress. I got out my diary and began to write in a shaky hand, *Dear God, help me to like her. Help her to like me.*

Three days later, I made another entry in my diary: *Dear God, I don't like her. There's no helping it. And I won't be welcome in David's home as long as she's there.*

I tried to make the best of it. I bought food that I thought David would like and made lunches for him. He ate them on the run. I gave up hope that he would have lunch with me and I began dropping the lunches off on his desk.

When I was invited along for dinner out, I watched Barbie drain one glass of wine after another. Wines are expensive in Canada. One of David's employees joked, "Barbie's on the wagon and David's pulling it."

She stopped by to see me one day. "I need some milk for David's cereal," she told me as she was leaving. David doesn't drink milk. When I gave it to her, her washed-out, acid-blue eyes shifted to the ceiling. "You're welcome to come up for a day or two. I mean, if you want."

Sure thing. I had given up on faith and hope. There went charity.

The one, thin blanket was completely inadequate. I froze during the nights and eventually caught a bad cold. I couldn't even get to the arts center to meet anyone.

One evening David came by with some warm blankets,

oranges, antihistamines. We had an evening like old times, listening to Mozart's Jupiter Symphony and playing Scrabble. I even won one game.

David's car was on the hoist and his bike needed repairs, so he had decided to call Barbie to ask her to pick him up on her way home. She arrived, smelling like a brewery.

"You've had a beer?" I asked.

"Two," she replied.

Just two? "Uh-huh. Let David drive."

The next day David, livid, accused me of putting her on the defensive.

"David, I don't like her," I blurted out. "She has no class, no culture, no warmth."

"You're an intellectual snob," he accused me, angrily.

"David, even if that were true, I would still learn to love her if I thought she were good for you."

A few nights before, I had waited hours for them to arrive to take me to dinner. Barbie's face was flushed. As I walked ahead of them to the car, I heard her sneer at him, "Mama's boy."

She ate and ran, off to a party—"at the ski resort where she works. She wanted me to go with her. I wanted to spend the evening with you, Ma."

Finally, after watching her consume five, six glasses of wine at dinner night after night, I asked David, "Does she have a drinking problem?"

He paused before he answered diplomatically, "I wouldn't know."

The last straw was the matter of Leo's records—Tchaikovsky,

Bach, Beethoven, Mozart—still in the carton in which I had sent them. The identification labels on the jackets had been removed. Over dessert one evening I spoke of the pleasure I was getting out of hearing Leo's old records again.

"They're not Leo's records. They're Barbie's," David told me.

"How could they be?" I asked him. "They're 78s, almost fifty years old. They're collectors' items. I sent them to you, David, because yours is the only permanent home in the family."

David's face hardened. He thrust out his chin. "They're Barbie's records. Ask her."

I turned to Barbie.

"They're my records," she said coldly.

"Barbie wouldn't lie," David said, looking at the floor.

Those records were as much hers as the lovely things she sometimes wore. "I got it from the L & F Store," she would brazenly tell me in response to a compliment. She was referring to the lost-and-found department at the ski resort where she worked.

Rather than love, than money, than fame, give me truth.

That evening when we reached the bungalow, David walked me in. "You don't give her credit for anything. She was the one who brought down the linens and dishes for you."

I told him about the threadbare linens, and I added, "As for the records, you yourself said she doesn't know anything about music."

After he left, I wrote tearfully in my diary: *I'll never come here again. I can't handle this pain.*

I tried to remain calm. I was leaving the next day.

In the morning, when David came to take me to the airport, Barbie had not come along. Neither of us spoke much. My throat was in a knot. There were no hugs or kisses when we parted.

I cried all the way home on the plane. When I got back to Los Angeles, sick in body, sick at heart, a routine checkup found that my blood pressure had become problematic.

For three awful weeks of sleepless nights and a racing pulse, I waited for the phone to ring. Finally I swallowed my pride and called him. "Why haven't I heard from you?" I demanded.

"Because you keep hanging up when Barbie answers."

"David, this is the first time I've called. I would never stoop to hang-up calls."

"Then who was it?" he wondered.

I thought I'd heard the last of Barbie when she moved out, leaving my son with no more than a "bye."

Another of David's friends had called her a kangaroo: always on the hop.

We lost something lovely and innocent that July. This trip was supposed to heal the rift. How could David include this selfish woman in our plans?

SUNDAY, JULY 22, YELLOWSTONE NATIONAL PARK, WY

Fifty miles beyond Cody we pull into a rest area. Yesterday's revelation has kept us silent all morning. After we wash up and David has unpacked some fruit, I confront him.

He shrugs. "She called and said she wanted to visit me, and I told her about this trip. She said since we were stopping in Yellowstone, she'd meet us there. Was I supposed to lie, Ma?"

"She sure can. If those weren't Leo's records, then where are his?"

David's patience is wearing thin. "I don't know. I have other cartons I haven't unpacked. For God's sake, stop nagging me!"

"She was just trying to control you," I tell him.

His body stiffens. "You're the one who's trying to control me! For forty years you've been trying to control me!"

"Stupid," I blurt out.

"Can't you ever just shut up?" he yells, his voice shrill and cracking.

"Take me to the nearest Greyhound station. I don't want to be around you anymore!" I shout back, pounding the table with my fist.

"I want my suitcase."

"Are you sure?"

"I'm sure."

David unstraps the suitcase and puts it down in the road in front of the station. He takes out some money.

"I don't want your money," I tell him. "I've got my VISA."

He follows me inside with the suitcase. I hand him the helmet. He looks at the board. "It's a three-hour wait for the bus to Los Angeles."

"I don't care."

It is five whole minutes after he leaves before I hear the engine start and the Dove roar off. I could die. Through my tears I read, or try to read, the schedule. Like he said, three hours and no ticket agent, no passengers, nobody around at all. I walk into the ladies' room, put my suitcase down, and cry until I'm gasping for air. I wash my face with cold water: Leo's remedy for the kids when they became upset.

When I look into the mirror, I see the same red, sodden face I saw when he died.

People are beginning to gather in the lobby. I seat myself on a bench and sit frozen, staring at my shoes. I sit this way for what seems an awfully long time. I look up at the clock once but don't see it. Then I hear a motorcycle pull up out-side. *A lot of motorcycles in this town, I mustn't think, mustn't imagine, it's too late now, this trip was supposed to be…*

Then I hear the door open, the sound of boots echoing over the flags of the lobby floor. Out of the corner of my eye I see boots, brown leather jacket and brown leather pants, and then the helmet.

When I look up, I'm trembling.

"We're getting a late start, Ma," he says, handing me back my helmet.

I'm clinging to the Dove once more, and the rain has let up. David speaks through the intercom. "I'll be taking back roads. There's a spectacular view from an old bridge. It takes us a bit out of our way. Is that all right with you?"

"Whatever you say, dear."

We reach the old bridge by way of an overgrown path. I need to stretch my legs, so David suggests we take a short walk first.

Walking silently side by side among the maples and spruce, the robins trilling in the trees, the croak of a bull-frog from a nearby pond, the piney fragrance again stirs to life one of those elusive memories.

"Once when you were a child, we were picnicking in a place like this, and you got lost. I was frantic. When we finally found you, you said, 'Whatsa matter? You were the ones who were lost.'"

David is smiling.

Here and there are pine seedlings springing from the dry earth, exposed by the footprint of some creature. I look back over my shoulder and there is the Dove near the old bridge. I cannot explain the respect and affection I have come to feel toward this machine. Could it be that we both have seen, and survived, better days?

The bridge is a weather-battered old thing, its rails broken, its timbers warped. Some two hundred feet below it, a river froths in the teeth of jagged rock.

"Stay here, Ma," David commands. And before I realize what is happening, he is starting across the bridge. Only now do I notice the warning sign: DANGER. CROSS AT YOUR OWN RISK.

"David," I shout after him, "Please come back!"

"Just wait where you are," he says calmly, continuing across the rickety bridge.

But I can't stay behind, and before I've completed the

thought, I'm stepping out onto the swaying slats.

"Ma! Are you crazy? Go back!"

The slats groan beneath my feet; there's no railing to hold onto. I shake with terror as I take a few more tentative steps toward him. By now I'm terrified. "David, please come back. Give me your hand."

Carefully, he makes his way back and grasps my out-stretched hand. I look up now and this makes me dizzy. I'm going to fall, I think, and drag him down into the rapids with me.

My heart is pounding as he guides me not back but onward across the rotten boards of the bridge so narrow that there is barely room enough for one to cross. "Watch out for the next one," he warns, his voice steady, calm. "Take slow steps. Careful, this one doesn't look good."

My eyes remain riveted to the creaking slats. "Slowly, Ma," he says, still calm, "We're nearly there."

When we've reached the other end, he stands surveying the view with admiration, oblivious to the danger he's just put us both in. "Spectacular!" He whoops once, we both listen for the echo, and then he pulls some coins from his pocket and flings them one after another to the water below, just as he did for the diving teenagers beneath the Brooklyn Bridge that long-ago summer.

No path picks up on the far side, only a shelf cut into a sheer rock wall. We must go back the way we came.

I let go of his hand, turn awkwardly, get on my hands and knees, and begin the trip back.

"Just relax, Ma. I'm right behind you," he's telling me. *David, get on your knees.* I try to speak but no words come out.

David crouches right behind me, ready to catch me if I go. *God, don't forsake us,* I pray. *Protect us both, but if you can't, hallowed be thy name anyway, thy will be done.*

As I crawl over the missing slats, my stiff fingers picking up splinters all the way, I can see the boiling abyss far below. When the next slat bends and cracks beneath one of my knees, David cries out, "Ma!"

Suddenly, and strangely, I too have become calm, self-possessed. I reach my hands for the next slat, bring one knee forward, then the other, until they meet my hands. I can hardly believe it when I cross the last slat and my hands touch thick tufts of grass and terra firma. I hold my breath as David nimbly dances across the last five slats and springs off the bridge.

The Dove weaves gracefully through the twists and turns of the mountain highway. *"We do the hokey-pokey and we turn ourselves around, that's what it's all about,"* I'm singing to the wind. I throw my arms about my pilot's waist, and for the first time on this long journey I hug him as we ride.

Although we'll be meeting Barbie in Yellowstone in a few hours, the prospect no longer, somehow, seems important.

We enter Yellowstone in a brief, torrential squall. David stops so that we can change into our rain suits. My hands are so cold I need David's help to do up the buttons.

The stone benches outside the Old Faithful Lodge are

empty. A man informs us that the famous geyser is due to spout in twenty minutes.

"You'd be more comfortable waiting in the lodge," David says.

"No, I'm fine here." I want to stay with him.

There are dozens of small geysers. When they erupt, the hot, heavy, fecund odor smells of lust and generation. I'm warmed momentarily by their steamy exhalations.

A buffalo ambles by, its heavy haunches swinging. DO NOT TOUCH THE BISON, signs warn. SOME VISITORS HAVE BEEN GORED BY THEM. "We'd better take cover in the lodge," David announces. "Old Faithful goes into action in a few minutes."

Inside, children press their noses up against the windows as the countdown begins. Five, four, three, two, one, and there it goes with a violent hissing, as eight thousand gallons of steaming water spew three hundred feet into the air. So much pent-up pressure, so beautiful in its release.

By now I have warmed up. We mingle with the crowd of tourists, many from distant countries and speaking German, French, Japanese. The girls all wear lots of makeup and shorts, their shoulders and round arms bare, their legs smoothly shaven; I have had my season of bare arms, shoulders, legs.

The lodge is vast and very impressive: tall river-rock fireplaces, gleaming polished wood, chandeliers, a grand vestibule, cozy alcoves. The concession stands diminish none of its charm.

David buys us two overflowing cups of ice cream.

"When are we meeting Barbie?" I ask casually between spoonfuls.

"In about an hour. We'll have an early dinner. I want to get to Ashton by tonight."

We take our cups to a table just vacated by a couple and their small child, who has been pulling a wad of gum from between her teeth. As soon as I slide into the seat, I realize she's left it behind—and these are my best black pants!

David rushes to the men's room, returns with a wet paper towel, and tries unsuccessfully to remove the gum. This inspires snickering from a nearby group of teenagers. "Did you know there's something on the back of your pants?" one of them says.

"Grow up, sonny," I tell him scornfully as we leave. Blow for blow.

The rain has stopped. We find a pay phone, call my sister to wish her happy birthday, then Mark, who thanks us three times for calling. I feel happy, good to have shared our momentary contentment with two other people.

As we walk through the lodge and back to the bike, my senses feel sharpened; I am amazed at my energy and grateful for everything, even the rain, even Barbie, oddly—grateful to be alive, healthy, and with my son in this beautiful place.

We wait for Barbie in front of the restaurant.

"It's a shame you haven't heard from Rachel," I say.

"Maybe you're right and she's met someone else," David says evenly. "I know I should have answered her letters sooner, but I wanted to think about what to write."

There is a long pause before he says, "I'd be glad just to have her friendship now."

Barbie arrives, acknowledges me with a nod, and throws her arms around David. Listening to her talk, it occurs to me that her voice is like her figure: flat, ironed out.

"Wine, Barbie?" David asks, smiling, when we've been seated.

"Yes, a bottle, that'd be neato," she says, sending a shiver of revulsion through me. It was a word she frequently abused.

While we wait for our food, Barbie addresses David as if I'm not there. "This man I'm living with, I don't know if I'll be going back to him."

"Why not?" David asks.

"He's kind of a bore. Actually, I had more fun with you."

"Oops!" I yelp, knocking over a full glass of ice water. "Sorry!" The busboy rushes over and mops the table.

"My station wagon needs work," Barbie says, brushing an ice cube from her lap. "I was thinking of bringing it up to you."

"Sure, bring it up. I'll take care of it."

"And how long will you be staying in Vernon, 'Ma?'"

I look her in the eye and smile: "I'm not sure. Maybe for good this time." I look over at my son. If it isn't precisely true, we both know it could be.

David's hand covers mine. We are beaming at each other

now. "I'm going to build a house for my mother next to mine."

"*Really?* Well, well. I see. Guess I'll be seeing both of you in Vernon then," she says uncertainly.

"I guess so," David says.

Barbie refills her glass to the brim, some red wine sloshing onto the white tablecloth.

This woman will never cause me hot flashes again.

The firm, tender pressure of a hand on my knee. I must have been nodding off again. David is rousing me; my helmet is touching his back.

I look up. The dusky sky has bronzed over with the setting of the sun. Through hooded eyes, I study my son's strong back shielding me from the wind. A memory of the scent of honeysuckle comes drifting back to me now, how it wafted through the open window on nights long ago as I lay singing him to sleep, my hand entwined in his thick, velvety curls. I have taken those precious days for granted.

It's growing late, but David is determined to reach Ashton tonight. The blinding glare of the oncoming headlights makes me glad I'm not the pilot. We're traveling fast, but I'm not afraid. Like another Dorothy, I've found some courage and some heart. Is it possible I have found a little wisdom too?

We reach Ashton after nine.

"Will you stop at a supermarket?" I ask David over the intercom. "I'm hungry."

"We'll try and find a restaurant later, Ma. More important that we get a room first."

Finding no vacancies along Main Street, we turn up an unpaved side street lined with log cabins but few signs. I am told to sit still on the heavily laden bike while David goes into an office. He returns with a young man in an undershirt, dark pants, and green visor, his acne-scarred face gaunt beneath the yellowing streetlight.

"All we got's a single," he says, looking me up and down in an unsavory way.

"Ma?"

Once before David and I were forced to share a bed as adults. He turned over and was asleep in seconds; I lay awake, awkward and uncomfortable.

We take the tiny room with the promise of a cot, which is duly delivered by the leering clerk. It barely fits, tight up against the door.

The room smells of fresh paint and new wood. There are no frills—no phone, not even a closet—but at least it's clean. David goes in search of a shower. I put on my green flannel nightshirt and lie across the bed. Our journey is almost over. How far have we come? I wonder.

David emerges from the bathroom shivering and pale, toweling his curly hair. "No hot water, Ma."

For no particular reason, I remember a very old joke. "David, do you know the one about the Jewish mother?"

He rolls his eyes. "How could I not?"

I ignore this. "A young man is asked by his girlfriend to go and cut out his mother's heart and bring it to her. He does. On the way back he trips and falls. The heart cries out, 'My son, did you hurt yourself?'"

David smiles. "That's a joke for dinosaurs, Ma."

"There's still a few of us around."

"I suppose the girl's name was Barbie."

"Never crossed my mind."

I'm too tired to get dressed and go back out for something to eat. Instead, we split the remaining yogurt bars.

I wonder now why David, who loves the classics so, has never unpacked and listened to Leo's records in all the time since I shipped them. But when I open my mouth to ask him, I say something else altogether.

"Thank you for not giving up on me."

I want to believe that one day I will learn to keep some things to myself, to think before I speak, but all my life there has been this need to talk everything out. I bury my face in the pillow.

David tenderly pulls the covers over me. "Sure, Ma. We're both still learning."

MONDAY, JULY 23, SUPERIOR, MT

This morning, I am awakened by a crowing rooster, a barking dog.

Outside in the parking lot, David is playing with the dog, black like his old dog, Marnie. "See how she jumps, Ma? Just like Marnie used to when I got home in the evening."

Marnie lived to the ripe old age of a hundred and twenty.

That's in dog years, of course. When she became too weak and incontinent to be left alone while David worked, he finally had to put her to sleep. That hurt him terribly.

David takes the map from the Dove's pocket and begins studying it. "Tomorrow we get to Spokane. My friend Andrew has pear orchards there. He's one person I think you'll like, Ma." After an hour or two at Andrew's, he tells me, we'll be heading for Ed's place, five hours from Spokane, to stay the night. From there it's only three hours to Vernon, the last leg of our journey home.

Home. I savor the word. David's house, with its newly varnished floors, the built-ins, the carpet I sent him, is the only real home I have now, one warmed by familial love. It has been two years since I was last there, and how I have missed it.

We ride deep into a valley along the timberline, on a wind-blasted road canopied by encroaching pine, spruce, fir. There is a stream running alongside, patches of green along its banks dotted with tiny wildflowers. There's very little traffic, and the weather is perfect. Time seems to have no meaning in this ancient place.

We pass a solitary rider on a bicycle. "That guy must be traveling cross-country," David tells me over the intercom. "See the huge bundle on the rear rack."

"On a bicycle? He's crazy!"

"Isn't that what they said about you?"

We cruise into Leadore, a little town right out of a western, with high porches and a real saloon with swinging doors. I wouldn't be surprised to find that it was actually a movie set.

There are two restaurants facing each other on opposite sides of the street. "Which of these two places do you like better?" I ask a plump woman in a pink dirndl crossing the street.

Seemingly pleased to help, she says, "They're both good. If you want a drink, try the Juicy Cow."

A cowbell clangs as we enter the restaurant. It's a cozy, pleasant place, with red-checkered cloths on the tables, the smell of fried fish heavy in the air. The old schoolhouse clock on the wall chimes.

We deposit our helmets at a window table, go wash up, then seat ourselves. Our waitress has scrubbed red cheeks and light-brown hair parted in the middle, braided, and charmingly coiled on both sides of her head. The aroma of the food is making my mouth water.

The waitress has brought us hot bread, jams, pickle, mustard, ketchup. "I'll get you some coffee," she offers. "Or would you prefer tea?"

"I think we both prefer tea," I tell her. David nods his approval.

Through the window across the street, we can see a boy of maybe ten scrutinizing the Dove, just like David when he was growing up, loving everything on wheels, knowing they would take him somewhere, never quite sure where.

David's eyebrows are working acrobatically as he reads the menu. "Turn-of-the-century prices too. Unbelievable."

"Order anything you want for the both of us," I tell him as I butter a piece of the homemade bread.

We will have the lima bean soup, tuna salad, and apple pie.

The sun is now shining brightly. "Baseball weather," I say. "I can't count the number of doubleheaders I sat through with your father. I'd hex the umpire, calling the pitches. Anyone who gambled on my predictions won."

"Take me out to the ball game…," I begin to hum.

A young girl in decidedly 90s garb puts coins in a jukebox, and discordant rock music shakes the knotty-pine walls. I groan and cover my ears.

David reminds me of the time he locked me in his room in Van Nuys to make me listen to the Tijuana Brass.

"That's different. I liked that."

"Scott Joplin was different too, once. You should listen with an open mind once in a while. You might find others that are different too."

David's sermon ends when the bicyclist we passed back on the road has rolled into town and parked his bike next to the Dove. He crosses the street and comes into the restaurant. He wears faded blue jeans and a light blue T-shirt. His hair is very blond and falls into his eyes. David greets him and they talk across the tables.

He is indeed riding cross-country, having already logged a thousand miles. "I gave up my wife and $60,000 a year to make this trip," he says.

His voice is huge for his slight frame, making me wonder if he was as thin as he is now when he started his journey.

"Best food I've had since Santa Fe," I tell David over our meals.

"I'll make us some great Mexican food when we get home," he promises.

"It's going to seem strange—almost as if it had been a dream—when this is all over and I'm sitting in my apartment again back in Los Angeles," I say.

David covers my hand with his. "I know, Ma. I'll miss you too."

I used to be embarrassed when my mother cried anytime one of us went away, more so as she grew older. Now, I have to fight back my own tears.

We sit quietly for a while before the check comes and we rise to leave. David tips $2.50 and I put down another dollar, just because I like the waitress.

On the way out, David gives the bicyclist his card, just in case he swings through Canada.

At the outskirts of town, David gets gas from a boy of twelve—working his way through elementary school, I assume.

"Great place!" David remarks. "That bicyclist was an interesting guy, wasn't he, Ma?"

"Just another adventurer," I say, then suddenly I feel a flush of shame: that was what Philip called me.

"Come on, Ma. He's got courage, lots of it, to cross the whole country on a bike! He'll make it too."

After we've been back on the road an hour or so, David's voice flickers to life in my ear. "Ma, the weather's ideal, and we've got an open road. How about a little adventure to tell your friends about when you're back at home?"

"I'm having an adventure, thank you very much!"

"I mean a *real* thrill, Ma. Wouldn't you like to experience going a hundred miles an hour on a motorcycle, just once in your life? Even if it's just for a short burst? This Dove is itching to fly!"

My mind is on my maker as I resign myself to Fate. I can die now, or I can die later. I shrug acquiescence. We ride along at cruising speed for a while, until we come up behind an old pickup truck. David accelerates to pass it, and he goes right on accelerating as we pull back in. The scenery blurs; the road seems awfully close. The noise intensifies, and the wind is trying to wrench the helmet off my head.

I remember the time when Mark—so solid and steady, so loathe to take risks—climbed on back of the Dove for "just a little ride." David had been going on about the magic and thrill of riding. When Mark got off, all he said was, "Safety thrills me!" I look over David's shoulder and glimpse the speedometer: the quivering needle hovers in the vicinity of 110 mph.

Like an amusement park ride that seems too short when you stand on the sidelines watching, but seems to last forever once it's your own insides getting homogenized, my full-throttle ride lasts, in truth, only three minutes. I have survived again.

Long shadows have overtaken the sun. The light fades first to a twilit lavender, then turns silver. I hug David tightly,

singing to myself merrily as the Dove scuds along like a child
skipping rope: I is for Idaho, M for Montana … One night
here before tomorrow's jaunt across the handle part of the
Panhandle State, W is for Washington, Andrew's farm, and
a feast of pears.

When it turns dark at last, the stars come out as if God
has signed his name across the heavens.

Barring an emergency, there will be no stops until we
reach Superior. I have only $7.13 left and a credit card.
David guesses he has just enough money to get us to Canada.
Still, we will not be camping out tonight.

I need to stop but see no rest area. I give David the two-
taps signal, which tells him to pull over. He does, halting in
a grove of trees, and hands me the flashlight.

After falling over a rotting log, then picking my way
through a troupe of giant toadstools, accompanied by a
whining chorus of persistent mosquitoes, I decide I cannot
perform here.

"It's the bugs, David," I call out.

"What about them?"

"I can't expose my tender flesh to these vultures."

"Use your hands," he calls back. "Just slap them away."

I suspect he has used the stop to good purpose.

"You've accomplished?" he asks delicately when I return.

I nod. I have accomplished.

Main Street, Superior, Montana. *No Vacancies*. Again, we try
a side street and find a small hotel. The night clerk is a

tired-looking man with a toothpick in his mouth, which he shifts from side to side compulsively, his pate bald but for a fringe of hair about his ears, which is gathered into a ponytail. His sandals slap the wooden stairs as he leads us up to our room: there are two double beds, two dressers, and a sink. The clerk yawns and scratches himself as we look around; the room is a bargain at eighteen dollars.

There is no one else on the floor, so we have the communal bathroom all to ourselves. Clean and just outside our door, it holds lingering odors of shaving cream, insect repellent, deodorant.

After my shower I dust myself generously with talcum powder, put on my nightgown, and sit down on my bed contentedly—it's always good to be on fresh clean sheets—gazing out the window at the silhouettes of mountains and trees against the starlit sky. A sense of completion has set in.

David returns looking refreshed by his shower and wearing the checked pajamas I bought him for his last birthday. "Tomorrow's our last day on the road."

He doesn't have to remind me. I throw him a kiss.

He reciprocates, and getting into bed, says, "You smell good, Ma."

"I'd better. It's all I've got, plus the seven dollars and thirteen cents."

"I still have some money," he says sleepily, the last word fading away on his lips as he drops off almost instantly.

That night, I have a dream: wearing a pale-blue dress, a wide-brimmed blue picture hat like one I wore at an Easter parade once when I was young, I am twirling about in slow motion to the tinkling of a xylophone. When I wake, the xylophone has turned to rain on the roof.

In my dreams, I am always young.

TUESDAY, JULY 24, SPOKANE / OROVILLE, WA

I've risen early, the more to savor the first light of morning and the cool air coming off the mountain, maybe the last fresh breath of air on this holiday from the routine violence reported daily in the *Los Angeles Times*.

In the bathroom, dressing in front of the mirror while David sleeps, I notice that the dark, deep-set appearance of my eyes has almost vanished. Studying my face in the mirror now, I see the part of it, and me, that I like best: my father's curly hair and high cheekbones. David too has inherited traits of his grandfather: the well-shaped head, and the gentleness.

The weather started out tranquilly enough this morning, but if I was foolish enough to believe it was going to stay that way, I haven't learned anything on this trip. As we ride out of Superior, the gale-force wind is a mad prankster trying to drag us off the road and over a cliff. This doesn't intimidate David, who's doing his usual 80 mph. Now coming this way, now that, the wind seems determined to screw off my head and the loose-fitting helmet. There is no one else on the highway insane enough to be out on a motorcycle; even the cars have slowed down.

"Ma," David responds to my insistent poking, "I have to go at least this fast just to get us up this hill!"

Then, somewhere in the panhandle of the Panhandle State, just before we reach the Washington border, we lose the wind and the air grows summery-mild and musky.

Outside Spokane, the land extends in every direction covered with orchards of Anjou pear, the branches heavy with low-hanging, ripening lobes of blushing fruit. It's too tantalizing, so I tap David's shoulder. He pulls off onto the shoulder of the highway and removes his helmet.

"I'd like to pick a couple of pears," I announce.

"No way, Ma. Hate to see you shot for a pear."

"Do I really look so pearlike?"

"No, I'd take you more for a peach." David puts his helmet back on. "You'll get all the pears you want at Andrew's," he says over the intercom as we lunge back onto the road.

The scenery here in this part of Washington is heart-stoppingly beautiful—or at least it strikes me so. All the loving energy of nature is concentrated in my heart today. The sensation is almost erotic. "David," I say into the intercom, "there must be such a place, a Fountain of Youth, which sends one back feeling rejuvenated, as if all things were still possible."

"That's great, Ma," he tells me. "Save a bite of that dream for me."

Then suddenly I'm standing up on the footpegs and

craning my neck. Just off the road, bent over her planting amid the welter of a parti-color flower garden, is an elderly woman, quite nude, wearing only a broad-rimmed straw sun hat!

I tap David on the shoulder and point. He looks, throws his head back, and laughs. "Down, Ma," he tells me, then speeds up.

It isn't until we come to a sudden stop in an orchard that I say to him as I climb off the bike, "David, that woman must have been crazy. Didn't you see her? She looked even older than me."

"Crazy like a fox, Ma," he says as he pulls off his helmet and leather gloves. "She stays cool that way. And she's visible. Haven't you complained about being invisible?"

We start walking up toward the house. I should have known the spectacle wouldn't faze him. "I remember when Robert Rabin stayed the night. You know what a prude he is. You came out of the bedroom followed by Michelle, both of you naked as newborns. What was so funny was that Michelle was eating an apple, remember? And had the presence of mind to offer Robert a bite."

We share a laugh. "You know, Ma, all those paintings of nudes hanging all over the house? I never told you, but when you weren't around, I'd bring my friends in to see them."

"You probably charged them too."

"Now, you know I've never been much of a businessman."

We've come to an expansive lawn before a house of brick and flagstone. A telescope pointed up at the sky stands sentry in front. A satellite dish on the roof mimics the telescope. A stream runs alongside the house and through a pretty little stand of trees. A card table stacked with cartons of the largest pears I have ever seen sits on the lawn. Next to the table, on an easel, sits a blackboard, scrawled with the words *Per jus 7¢ a glas.* The seven is written backwards. Minding the store are two little girls dressed in pink and yellow pinafores and holding identical dolls. There is an odor of burning leaves on the breeze.

David flashes them a big smile. "Hello. Is Andrew around?"

"That's my grandpa," says the older of the two girls. "Want me to call him for ya?"

"Not before we do some business. We'll have two glasses of juice and a couple of pears, please."

Delighted, the girls each pour a paper cup full of juice from a pretty Chinese vase. The younger one allows the vase to slip between her fingers with an "oops," spilling juice all over the table as the vase breaks. David and I help them clean it up with some paper towels, then give them a dollar apiece, which they deposit in a King Edward cigar box. They are obviously thrilled by the windfall.

Andrew appears. He is tall and slender, with a thatch of white hair, clad in farmer's gray overalls. There is a winning quickness of motion and an elegance about him. He and David hug before David introduces us. "Meet Dr. Swanson."

"Plain Andrew will do," he says, offering his hand. "I see you've already met my sales team."

"Hello," I say, taking his hand, feeling suddenly shy. Andrew is British, with an intonation worthy of the BBC.

"Where's the boat you wrote me about?" David asks, looking around.

"Needs a spot of work. You'll be seeing it soon enough. I'll be bringing it up to Vernon in a couple of days." He takes a photo from his billfold and hands it to David. "My first sailing boat," he explains, looking at me.

"Beautiful," David declares, and hands the photo to me: Andrew standing on the foredeck, in white turtleneck, white pants, white shoes.

"Handsome," I say.

"Me or the boat?" Andrew wonders, eyes twinkling.

David was right: I do like Andrew, instantly.

"How's the car?" David asks.

"Not well, I'm afraid. Makes this choking, throttling noise."

"Lemme take a look."

"Heavens no, you're on holiday, David."

"It's all right. Give me the keys."

David darts to the garage, the girls giggling after him, and I feel awkwardly left alone. "I'm sorry about the vase," I say, at a loss for anything else.

"It's only a vase," he observes. After several moments of silence, he continues, "I lost my wife not quite a year ago. I still haven't got over it. I hope it becomes easier."

This unexpected revelation oddly enough relieves my shyness. "I know how you feel. After my husband passed away, I went to the ocean every day. I used to sit for hours, just watching the waves. That was the only time I felt any peace. Does the sailing help?"

"That's why I bought the boat. My wife and I used to rent a boat every summer near David's home. That's how we met your son, out on the lake. My wife was very fond of him, as am I. Sorry, I'm forgetting my manners. May I offer you some tea? The children and I baked some scones—from a mix," he adds, apologetic.

I follow him to the kitchen, large like a farm kitchen, white and blue, full of greenery. I sit while he puts the water up to boil. He's very precise about the amount of tea. He sets out milk, sugar, and scones in a wooden basket.

While the tea steeps, we make small talk. "Once in my youth I worked for a tea company in London. I understand that you're an artist."

"That's right, although not professionally. I haven't actually done any painting in a while. I hope to do some in Canada," I tell him, feeling more at ease now.

"My father was an artist too. Nothing was more important than my father's painting. We were constantly being warned by my mother, 'Quiet now, your father's painting.' A feature article about him appeared in your *Better Homes & Gardens* and he became famous overnight. He eventually divorced my mother, couldn't go on with us, he said. Married a television actress—you've probably heard the story before? Anyway, his new wife wore a mountain of makeup. My mother never wore any, my father didn't like it. Success changes people, it seems?"

Andrew serves the tea in Wedgwood china. "It's delicious,"

I say, avoiding the subject of his father. I've made the connection: a fine designer with a fine sense of color, but no passion.

"Do you mind if I put on some music?" he asks now, already up and on his way to the next room.

"I'd love it," I say.

It's a Strauss waltz. Involuntarily, I find myself on my feet and following the music when Andrew returns and extends his arms, and suddenly I'm dancing again, really dancing, with a man. My awareness of myself as a woman in a woman's body comes rushing back to me.

David walks in on us and stops at the doorway, unable to decide if he should be embarrassed. Andrew and I move apart.

"That was quick," I say.

"Just a carburetor adjustment."

"Aren't you going to join us?" Andrew asks.

David jerks his thumb over his shoulder. "I promised the girls a ride on the Dove. I hope that's all right?"

"I think so. But what about some tea, David? Or would you prefer cider?" Andrew is already at the refrigerator door, retrieving a pitcher of cold cider.

"No thanks, Andrew."

He's in a hurry again.

"You sure? But you just got here."

"No time. We still have a long ride to Oroville."

"I'd like to take you and your mother out to dinner," Andrew says.

"We'll see you in Vernon," David says.

"Won't you finish your tea?" Andrew asks me.

"I'd rather finish the dance."

We smile at each other.

"Well then, I hope that one day soon I can offer you some of my carrot cake. No mix," he winks and smiles.

"That would be wonderful."

"You will be at David's?"

"Until Thursday."

"Then, in that case, I must be sure to be there by Tuesday, so that we can all spend a whole day on the water."

David gives each of the girls a quick ride through the orchard. They, and David, love it; the girls squeal with delight.

After warm farewells, we watch Andrew walking the girls, hand in hand, back to the house. David says, "Great guy. That man knows how to get on with his life. I'll bet he's remarried by next year."

Andrew and I are members of the same club. No one can take away the love we each had once. And while no one can bring it back again, either, we both know there is still the possibility of joy to be found in those surprises waiting just around the corner.

"Did you meet any men?" my friends will ask when I get back to L.A. "Yes," I'll tell them with a shrug, but they met David's mother, not a woman. Andrew will remain my secret.

The wind lays a gentle hand on my face; the sun is shining

brightly, making everything look crisply etched. I feel as if there is indeed a God, and he's taking friendly notice of me.

After three weeks and more than four thousand miles of nomadic wandering, with still the prospect of a few days of the tranquillity of David's mountain retreat, I haven't felt this young in years. With hours to go before we reach Ed's, I sit back in the saddle and begin taking stock of my experiences on the road. In sum: all my life I've sought others' attention; this trip has forced me to accept the simple reality that one cannot always be the center of attention.

I wonder if I will be able to tolerate my return to the heat, haze, and smog of Los Angeles.

We glide off the highway and into a Denny's parking lot. The welcoming aroma of fresh coffee makes me so hungry, I'm tempted momentarily to order bacon and eggs, but I've promised myself to stay on my best behavior. David orders pancakes and real maple syrup; he should know better. I decide on oatmeal and a short stack, much better for me. The trip has taken inches off my hips, even as it has added a whole new dimension to my life.

"David," I say, laughing, when the waitress has gone, "do you know you have a five o'clock shadow and it's only four o'clock? I remember once when you were three or four, you wouldn't let me wash your face. You said, 'Butsy Ann won't recognize me.'"

The lines of David's face crinkle with amusement. "She was all of five. My first love, an older woman."

"You were so cute. Where do all those cute kids go?"

David covers my hand with his. "Ma, I think I understand how you must have felt when I left home the first time."

"You were only seventeen, darling."

He smiles ruefully. "At the time you seemed to me just…"

"Bitchy?" I help.

After we stop laughing, David says, "Now maybe you can understand what these trips mean to me?"

There's an obese man sitting opposite us, cracking his knuckles. He's pretending to read a newspaper; his marshy brown eyes watch us askance. I conclude that he's just lonely. Loneliness is the very devil. When Leo was alive, I didn't know the meaning of the word. His passing crippled me with loneliness, to the point where I no longer had the will even to paint.

The food arrives and I very sparingly butter my pancakes. David is still consulting his map. We are going to take the Gifford ferry across Franklin Roosevelt Lake (which is not really a lake but the bulging waistline of the Columbia River). From there, Oroville is still a couple of hours away, but David says we should reach Ed's place on schedule.

Back on the Dove I am standing up on the footpegs to stretch my legs. *Thy wind, thy wide gray skies…* I want to hold this whole land in my arms, from the snow-banked mountain peaks down to the lakes and streams of the river valleys.

David signals me to sit: "Enough with *The Sound of Music*."

Behind two dozen cars inching forward eagerly in the line

for the ferry, deep-green, sweet-smelling Gifford reminds me of my vacations in the Catskills.

Aboard at last and pulling away from the moorings, we can see beyond the sibilant water foaming about the hull into a lake so clear, fish are visible deep below the surface.

Watching a group of elderly women on deck banter among themselves reminds me of something I meant to tell him. "David, I've made arrangements with the Neptune Society."

David looks at me disapprovingly. "I don't want to hear about that, Ma. Eat healthy, think healthy, stay healthy."

And I'll live forever? I refrain from adding.

He speaks as he focuses his camera on me with the lake in the background. "Someday you'll live with me in Vernon."

"And I'll nag you. I can't help it—I'm genetically programmed to nag."

"That's a cop-out, Ma. You can always suppress that gene."

I have measured my time here on the back of the Dove not by the watch face or calendar, but in images: rolling farm-land dotted with stock, a woman in a green pantsuit stretching up like a praying mantis to hang her laundry, a cordon of fishermen saluting a rippling lake with their poles, the green thatch of a cornfield, wide pastures that hold the sunlight like bowls of marmalade, a grouse flapping its wings and mimicking my morning stretches.

I enjoy every moment of it now while I can; soon enough

I'll be back yawning my way through my daily routines.

Or maybe I really will start painting again.

The overture to our arrival in Oroville opens with more orchards, shouting children. This segues into the grounds of an old schoolhouse, a horse running loose on someone's front lawn, then finally Ed's house, freshly painted an ultra-white.

Ed has been expecting us. His round, bald head nods up and down as he opens the garage door and David drives right on in, parking the bike next to a restored Model T Ford. A stalwart truck of the same era stands on the other side of the car.

Smiling ear to ear, Ed and David hug, slap each other on the back. The first thing David does is take out his camera. "Ma, Ed, in front of the car?"

Ed leans with his small, broad hand on the car's hood. I jump up on the running board. "It was a great vintage, this car and I," I say.

David snaps the picture and lowers the camera. "The car's worth more, Ma. At least, Ed can get more for it."

I take the riposte in stride. "Guess this old heap can't command the price she used to."

Ed leads us into the house—spartan and neat. The only signs of ostentation are the several large antique pieces.

"You'll want to wash up, I suppose," says Ed. "And there's some cold fruit juice I just made."

The juice turns out to be a blend of fruits, rich as a liqueur. David tells Ed that we are taking him out for dinner. I wonder if David has enough cash left. Our accounting methods are very different: I always know what I have down to the penny; he deals in ballpark figures, rounded numbers. He probably has more than he needs.

Ed is plainly happy to see David; the smile has not left his cherubic face since we arrived. He hands David the car keys. "Test drive the truck for me."

I climb into the back, stretch out, settle back, fold my arms over my chest, close my eyes. The truck's smell of freshly cut wood and old leather acts as a tranquilizer.

When I become aware of what sounds like water running over rocks, I sit back up. In the distance are reddish mountains. We pass a few farms, and then we're back in town.

"Smooth as a baby's bottom," pronounces David as we all get out.

"No plastic parts in the Model T," Ed beams.

Ed has directed us to a good Mexican restaurant where the owner knows him well and greets him in Spanish. Ed introduces David and they all chatter eagerly. The restaurant owner is quite handsome; he has thick black hair and wide shoulders; he swaggers when he walks. When they all begin to laugh, David looks at me and I wonder what they're talking about.

(Later David explains, "I was telling him how Louis, my friend from school, taught you to greet his father in obscene Spanish." That wasn't funny, I remind him.)

By the time we've eaten and driven back to Ed's, I'm asleep

on my feet. Ed spreads a heavy Mexican blanket on the living room floor in front of the picture window. We lay our sleeping bags out, and Ed says good night and heads off to bed.

We lie quietly side by side for a long period. The moon is full and the room is eerily lit up and dreamlike. Though I'm exhausted, now that I'm lying down, I can't sleep, not yet. There's still something I want to tell my son before this journey is over.

"David, are you awake?" I whisper.

"If you want me to be, I am," he whispers back.

"I want you to be, thanks. I know that I've been tired and bitchy, but I want you to know what an unforgettable experience this has been for me."

He sits up and looks at me. "There's something I want to say to you too, Ma." The moonlight captures the strong line of his cheeks and chin. He pauses, hesitating before he finally says, "I felt like hell when I left you at the bus station. The trip went flat for me. The fun was gone."

"Thank you for telling me that. I never would have known. You know when you go silent on me and walk away, I feel so abandoned."

"Ma, you never give me a chance—"

"What do you mean? David, the Messiah could come and go before you answer me."

He exhales. "Do you want to talk, or do you want me to talk?"

"Okay, I'll shut up. Talk."

He starts slowly. "You despise my friends."

"Not all of them," I'm quick to object. "But you *are* careless. You make friends with some terrible people who just want to use you."

He flops down and turns his back on me.

"David, I'm sorry. Please. I'm trying. David?"

Then he sits back up. "First of all, don't raise your voice. You'll wake Ed. Second, Ma, you have no right whatsoever to approve or disapprove of my friends."

The tone of his voice clobbers me. My heart is thumping painfully. I'm hurt, very hurt, and I'm beginning to cry. I say, "How disloyal can you be? I simply don't understand how you can take the side of people who deceive you, who lie to you and still call themselves your friends. I'm your mother, David. You should trust me."

There is a brief interval while we both stop to listen for sounds of Ed stirring. Then David says, his voice quivering, "Ma, I'm a grown man."

"Tell that to my blood pressure," I retort, immediately ashamed of this line of attack, unable once again to help myself, thinking what I really need right now is an ice pack and a double margarita.

I can hear Ed moving around now. I am probably keeping him awake, but I can't control my sobbing. The words just spill out: "Well, say it, for God's sake! Something's bothering you. Something's always bothered you. Something more than my disapproval of your friends."

"You really want to know?"

"Yes."

"Really?"

"Yes!"

His Adam's apple is bobbing. He wants to speak, but can't. My whole body is seized by a trembling while I wait for him to answer me, finally, in a voice so low I can barely understand him: "Okay, listen. When I was growing up, you were never there when I got home from school. You were always too busy. Remember Benny, the bully across the street? Remember how he was beating me black and blue, and you never noticed? I was terrified to walk home from school. My teacher had to tell my own mother what was happening to me."

"I remember," I answer him softly, my heart thudding away, my breathing shallow. I'll let him talk, have his say (he'll never repeat it), clear the air, the adult avenging the injustice to the child, and breaking my heart.

"You know, I couldn't wait for you to get home so that I could read you my compositions. But when you finally did, you never had the time. You always said, 'I'm busy. We'll do it later, David.' But we never did. You never knew ... never ... how jealous I was when you started teaching art to the other kids. It was like something was over between us. Like I wasn't your son anymore."

He pauses, strangled by the words. "I used to enjoy getting sick. You dropped everything to take care of me. That was the only time I could be sure you loved me."

He chokes up. I wait quietly for him to regain control. "The reason ... the reason I asked you to come along was that I wanted us to be close, to be like friends, like that summer in Brooklyn." He's been gesturing angrily, pointing his finger at me; now he takes a deep breath and folds his hands in his lap before he goes on, haltingly. "And … and I wanted you to know how I felt … how much I'm enjoying my life, Ma."

He looks at me intently now. "Why can't you just be glad that I'm happy and enjoying my life?"

Stunned by his candor, I don't know what to say. I never thought we—*he* would ever be talking this way, so I let him go on. "You must know why I never call you when I'm on the road."

I nod. Yes, I understand. Now.

The sounds from Ed's room have stopped. A horse snorts and neighs somewhere not far off. I can feel the breeze coming in through the open window, cooling my wet cheeks. David is holding his hand out, in it a handkerchief like a white flag. "Could you be a little less my mother and a little more my friend?"

In my heart, I'm saying, *Impossible! I can't stop being your mother!* Even if I've been a lousy one: a self-centered feminist before that became the prevailing fashion. Being a parent is a life sentence, I'm tempted to tell him. But instead I reach out, take the handkerchief in one hand, then with the other, his hand in mine. "I'll try, David. I promise."

David presses my hand, kisses me good night, kisses away the sting of my tears, making me feel cleaner, lighter.

As we lie side by side, I am transported back to those summer days when the fragrance of honeysuckle came in through the windows and I could run my hands through the curls of my slumbering five-year-old and sing to him.

"I'm sorry I didn't breast-feed you," I confess, softly.

"That's all right, Ma," he says just as softly, then chuckles. "You know, I have my business and my home. I don't need a lot of money. Even if you're right, and my friends are using me, they must need what I have more than I do. What if I am too generous—who do you think taught me to be that way?"

His words are a revelation. "I'll be damned if I didn't give birth to an angel," I say.

"Just don't be clipping my wings," he says, laughing now.

But it's true: his friends may not love him enough for his generous spirit, but mine do. Isn't that all that should matter to me? Isn't that the grin on the face on the other side of the coin? I'm the one who should be thankful.

"David, I forgive you," I tell him.

"And I forgive you, Ma." And now we're both chuckling, and then we're laughing. And I feel like I'm floating over the rooftops of a Chagal, as the moon slides out of view and then back with a wink, just as Leo used to wink at me. Love can be, quite literally, funny.

Before we turn over to go to sleep, I reach out, cradle David's face in my hands, and tell him, "You are so, so dear to me."

WEDNESDAY, JULY 25, VERNON, BC

When I open my eyes, I realize instantly how deliciously deeply I've slept.

David is already up. Right off, he hands me a big vitamin C tablet. "Here, chew this."

I clear my throat before I ask, "Will it make me young and beautiful again?"

"You're already beautiful, Ma. Just can't guarantee young."

This morning he wears his leather pants and a pink T-shirt bearing his business logo: two bears in a bear hug. He's looking very fresh and much younger than his years. It occurs to me that I have never done a portrait of him. Now I'm itching to start one.

"Looking good this morning, Ma."

"Sure about that?" Lately I've been glad my face is right where I can't see it.

When I finish showering and dressing, I make my entrance. Ed is saying to David, "I like your shirt."

"That's good, because I've got two just like it for you: a pink and a blue."

With the number he gave away at the rally, I'm surprised David has any left. I say nothing, deciding—just to get myself into the habit—that it's none of my business.

"Hey, hope we didn't wake you last night," David thinks to say now.

Ed is gracious about it. "I sleep better when I have friends in the house." There is sadness in his voice.

Ed hails from Vernon. I visited once with his parents, in the same house where they had lived for most of their lives. Evidence of Ed's mother's needlepoint work was everywhere, from the "God Bless Our Happy Home" sampler on the wall, to the doilies and embroidered pillows scattered on the sofa and easy chair. They were kind, uncomplicated people. I sat down on a pink stuffed dog lying on the easy chair and quickly jumped up, expecting a yelp of pain. (What could I have been thinking? A *pink* dog?!)

Waiting out in the front yard till breakfast is ready, I sit swinging in an old tire strung from a tree limb. Ed is alone, his parents in Vernon dead now; he's the last of his line, as cut off from his neighbors as the old horse (the one I must have heard last night) standing all alone there in its corral. I feel lucky that I still have my two boys, and my vivid memories of Leo.

"Tacos are ready," David has come out to announce. Tacos for breakfast? Why not? Another first. David gives me one last big push in the swing before I dig a toe into the grass, extricate myself, and follow him into the house.

Within a half hour of leaving Ed's farm, we have crossed the Canadian border.

My helmet is touching David's back when he nudges me awake. I massage his back, then he rubs my knee, as we cruise alongside a lake, on its shore a dock with long red canoes tied up, like the one David owns. We are almost home.

Vernon has grown from a population of seven thousand at the time of David's arrival to seventy thousand today. It's a quiet, sedate sort of town blessed with mountains, lakes, and rivers; it doesn't lack for the civilized amenities of a good library and a cultural center for the performing arts.

As we pass through, the great clock over the town square is striking twelve.

David's home is up Silver Star Mountain, mantled in evergreens, pine, and blue spruce, redolent, this time of year, of wild berries. One day soon I will paint this mountain. I'll start with charcoal, sketching out its old barns, fields, trees, and familiar faces, then wash the canvas in cadmium yellows, reds, ultramarines, viridians, cerulean blues—a testimony of all the colors gathered and hoarded, saved up from my great adventure.

Seven miles up the mountain, David stops off at the battery of red mailboxes. His eyes shine when he finds a letter among the overflow of his uncollected mail: "It's from Rachel."

"Well, open it," I say.

He shakes his head. "Not now. It's enough to know she's still a friend."

David brings the Dove to rest in the woodshed, where firewood has been cut and stacked for the winter season—harsh, but also the loveliest season in this neck of the Canadian woods.

When we have both stiffly dismounted and removed our helmets, David places a fond hand on the heap of firewood, pleased to be home and already prepared for the coming winter. I recall Thoreau's dictum: *While I enjoy the friendship of the seasons, I trust nothing that can make life a burden for me.* My son has found his Walden Pond.

David looks fondly at the Dove. "Good friend. Good, good friend," he pronounces, placing his hand on the worn seat.

"We made it, David," I say, gratefully, laying my hand over his. *And thank you for bringing us home safe and sound,* I add, a silent benediction.

I follow him out of the shed, and we go, accompanied by birdsong, up the curved stone walkway to the house. The archway over the front door is bathed in golden light. It's only late July, but already I can feel the season beginning to turn.

When he opens the door, the cat, sleek and well cared for in his absence, springs into his arms. He studies my reaction now as I follow him in and peer about, spellbound, at this familiar room tinted blue, red, green from the light filtering through the stained-glass windows that I have so missed and so often dreamed of seeing again.

"Is there any place more beautiful?" David says.

There can be no question. Nothing is more beautiful than this. Nor holy.

May your union be blessed with children to sustain you in your old age. And so they do, my sons: my bread and sunshine.

EPILOGUE

There has hardly passed a day when I haven't been re-minded of my great good fortune for the gift of that magical, life-restoring summer—the Indian summer of my life. Once back in Los Angeles, the memories of that month on the road with David and the Dove nourished and sustained my spirits. And to make sure, this time, that I wouldn't lose those memories—as I nearly had the recollected history in-spired by that trip six summers ago—I began setting them down in my diary, retrospectively, not so much as a memoir for my own posterity, but as a reminder to myself of how much I still had to live for.

Thus, the spirit remained willing. It was the flesh that proved weak—inevitably, I'm afraid: after an operation that left me nearly unable to walk, I became a shut-in. For the first time in my adult life, I was unable to care for myself. Humiliated, my spirits, understandably, began to sink.

It was during this time that it occurred to me that, high spirits or low, good or failing health aside, none of it might very well have happened at all. I too might have dismissed David's invitation as absurd, much as those unnumbered friends, family members, neighbors, and observers must have, who wondered what *a woman of my age* could be thinking, traipsing around the country on the back of a motorcycle!

But the motorcycle, the perilous mountain highways, and the rally had been hardly the point; it might just as easily—or just as uneasily!—have been an elephant, a jungle, and a Buddhist pilgrimage. The elements—the props, if you will—of the journey were merely the catalysts of the adventure. The adventure itself, its essence, was still here, in my heart and the tremulous handwriting.

Luckily, after the operation, David rushed to my side: dropped his work, left his wife and lovely two adopted children in Canada, and came down to spend two weeks, taking care of me. With his help, every nook, corner, and crevice of my home gleamed, the salads stayed green, the dishes sparkled, and my spirits rose again. David and I spent the days swapping the epic stories of our wandering together. At night, packing me into the car—my motorcycling days were now also part of my storied past—David would drive me up into the hills above the city, to look at the mountains purple in the distance, God's inimitable, unrepeatable creation, the eternal stars above outshining the ephemeral ones dwelling in the haze below.

"I love you, Mom," he said to me on one of those drives. Had I not taken a chance that summer, I might never again have heard those precious words. I might very well have taken all those needless fears and anxieties, the bitterness and rage at all the injustices of this world, the disappointments with my fellow creatures, to an early grave.

Anyone can be too young to die. By my reckoning, God collected my Leo much too early. He won't get me very soon, not without the good fight. My spirits remain high. I see to that. Or the boys do. When I forget my resolve, become glum, and backslide into my propensity for kvetching, Mark, my other staff, continues to tease me, saying things like, "Ma, how come you remember everything so well?"

I just laugh, and the sun comes back out.

And so, in my not-so-old old age, my sons remain my daily bread. As for the rest of my spiritual diet, I paint my portraits, make my diary entries, read my Faulkner, enjoy my hard-won peace of mind. Found that hound, bay horse, and turtle dove: their trail leads here.